CW01390917

This edition published in 2014 by Amazon

Copyright © 2014 Warren Karno

P O Box 35-275
Browns Bay
Auckland
New Zealand

ISBN-13: 978-1494832766

All rights reserved. No part of this publication may be reproduced, stored in a retrieval system or transmitted, in any form or by any means, electronic, mechanical, photocopying, recording or otherwise without the prior written permission of the author.

Cover design by Warren Karno.

Disclaimer: Whilst this story is inspired by some actual events, the author stresses the characters, companies and institutions named are purely fictitious and any resemblance to anyone living or dead is purely coincidental. The purpose of the story is of entertainment value only.

VOYAGE OF A VINDI BOY

By

WARREN KARNO

Published By:

Warren Karno on Amazon.com

Copyright 2014 by Warren Karno

* * *

For glossary of terms, see back pages.

Acknowledgement

This book has been very much inspired by the efforts of Roy Derham M.B.E. of Fareham Hants and an ex-Vindi lad. His persistence in forming the TS Vindicatrix Association helped keep the spirit of the old ship alive and many shipmates have met again as a result. An estimated 12,000 are still alive today of which one-third are in the 'colonies'.

This is a true story. Only names have been changed to protect the guilty.

* * *

Preface

The description of Joseph Lawson's first ship – a large white liner bound for South America – was the sweetest music to his ears. It was everything a sea-struck fifteen-year-old could desire.

Imagine his dismay when he first saw the Princess Tara in reality. Rather than being a white liner, it was an old, black-hulled cargo boat, crewed by the motliest collection of seamen possible.

But Joe - a graduate of the TS Vindicatrix sea-training school, berthed at Sharpness – soon realised that the most important thing was being at sea, regardless of the ship, and that even among the motley, he could still find supportive company.

Voyage of a Vindi Boy is a dramatic, informative, and at times poignant account of a young lad's Merchant Navy experiences in the early 1950s. Not an advised read for mothers! Or those of a prim disposition.

* * *

Table of Contents

* * *

CHAPTER 1

'Run away to sea, young man'

The fine drizzle went almost unnoticed. That there was no money in my pocket seemed unimportant, that it was 2am on a cold park bench in Hull meant only that I had another seven hours or so to wait. In the meantime I could visualise the tropical beach, palm trees of the Caribbean gently swaying high above my heads as I lay on the white sand, my back soaking up its warmth, my hand picking up the fine sand and allowing it to fall through my fingers.

'Oh yes, who have we here young fella?' I broke out of my reverie to find a large policeman standing over me.

'Joseph Lawson, sir.'

'And what brings you to this deserted park at this time of night?' He shone his torch in my face, then down at my old suitcase, its label bearing my home address in Nottingham.

'I'm going to join a ship,' I replied proudly.

Sitting on the bench beside me, the sergeant enquired further: 'And where are you planning to sleep tonight?'

I was far too excited to have given this triviality much consideration, and anyway I had less than a shilling. 'Well, I thought I could stay here, sir,' I countered somewhat meekly

'You can come along with me. We'll see if we can get you a hot drink and something to eat.' The policeman stood and picked up my case, which was held together with twine and was surprisingly heavy. Large knots were everywhere; clearly the work of a young traveller and not an experienced seaman.

'How old are you, Joseph?'

'Fifteen and a quarter years, sir,' I answered.

'Is this your first time away from home?'

'No, I have been working up in Harrogate for a year.'

'Oh, have you now. And doing what may I ask?'

'Well, I started as a page boy, then became an assistant waiter,' I told him, trying to sound grown-up.

'Well, then you're old enough to realise that it's not a good idea for a young chap like you to be out alone at this hour. I take it you've no money to pay for a hotel room?'

'No, sir.'

'That's what I thought,' he said grimly as we walked through the sleeping city streets. 'Does your mother know you're here?'

'Oh yes! She helped me a lot.'

'At this time of night?'

'Well, the train connection at York was delayed and didn't get here till almost eleven o'clock.'

'So where were you going to stay?'

'I don't know, I thought the ship.'

'You must be joking! Do you know how far it is from here?'

'No, sir.'

The streets of Hull were almost deserted, shiny from a recent shower and the seemingly constant drizzle. In the distance, car tyres whistled on the wet surface. Before long the policeman led the way down the side of a large building and, much to my surprise, opened a window.

'Come on, young 'un, up you go.' He easily lifted me over the windowsill and passed my case through after me. When we were both inside and the window had been closed, he switched on the light. I realised this policeman knew his way around and must have done this sort of thing before.

'Who lives here?' I asked in a hushed voice.

'This is the Seaman's Mission – you are a seaman, aren't you?'

To be called a seaman by a policeman felt really good. 'Oh yes, sir, though I'm a steward seaman. A senior steward actually,' I added, remembering the two stars on my uniform sleeve from the Vindicatrix sea school.

'Well, get this down you, Mr Senior Steward Seaman,' and he thrust a two-inch thick peanut butter bread slice into my hand. We were in the kitchen of the Flying Angel Mission to Seamen, a regular stop-off point for Sergeant Rigby. On many occasions, the commercial port of Hull offered up lost or drunken sailors to whom the 'Angel' provided a welcome refuge against the rain or icy winds that blow in from the North Sea. The policeman grinned at the sight of me with peanut butter from ear to ear, and in no time he handed me a large, steaming mug of cocoa.

'Here, wash it down with this. Then let's see if we can find you a bed. We old Vindi boys have to look after each other. Isn't that right?' he said with a warm smile.

'You're an ex-Vindi boy! Then how did you become a policeman?'

'Now that's a long story. C'mon – let's get your head down.'

He showed me to a room with four beds in it, three of which were not in use.

'Get those wet clothes off and get in here,' he said, pulling back the covers on one of the beds.

I took off my navy blue serge uniform, shirt and socks, starting to fold them and put them on the chair beside the bed.

'Oh, no, you don't,' said the sergeant, scooping up my clothes. 'I'll put these in the kitchen over the Aga. They'll be dry in the morning.'

I jumped between the cold sheets and curled up to keep warm. 'Thank you,' I said, looking up at the sergeant's face. His rather severe appearance was due, I thought, more to his large size and impressive uniform than to his facial expression. His eyes were kind and the corners of his mouth quivered a little before breaking into a smile that spread all over his face.

'Good night son. Good luck tomorrow.' He switched off the light and quietly closed the door behind him.

The dark room was filled with silence, so I closed my eyes and thought what a great dad the sergeant would make. Still, he probably had his own children. I wondered what my dad was like and where he might be. The only thing I knew was he didn't want to be with my mum and me. Maybe it was good that I never had the chance to know him. You couldn't miss someone you didn't know. I bet the sergeant would never leave his family.

The following morning a hand shook my shoulder. 'Here's your clothes, kid. The padre's just brought them in.' The voice belonged to my roommate, who was almost dressed. His weather-beaten face looked like it had been at sea for years.

'Come on. Shift yourself if you want some breakfast.'

I quickly jumped into my warm, dry clothes, stuck my head under the cold tap above the basin and, combing my hair, said, 'Ready when you are.'

'You straight from the Vindi?' he asked, glancing at my uniform.

'Yes. Just joining my first ship,' I said, following him down the passage into the dining room. We were both given a plateful of eggs, bacon and fried bread, then we found a table to sit at.

'What ship have you got?' he asked.

'The Princess Tara. Do you know it?'

'Of course I know it. It's a large white liner, does the South America run – or is it Australia? I'm not sure which, but you'll love it!' he said, smiling. 'Now, are you going to get the teas in?'

This was the sweetest music to my ears: the perfect accompaniment to my egg and bacon. I wanted him to tell me more, but he was in a rush with his food and I didn't like to interrupt. Then he had to go. 'Good luck, kid,' he said and left.

After breakfast, I went to the office to explain that I had no money, for although the kind policeman had said it would be okay, I wanted to say thank you. Much to my surprise, I was confronted by the padre. He looked over the top of his frameless glasses and explained that the sergeant had left a note telling him that I had no money. The padre gave me a postcard depicting the Hull 'arboretum', suggesting that I write and tell mum I was safe and sound. I could hand it back to him for posting before I left to find my ship, he said.

'Dear Mum. The Princess Tara is a big white liner and it's going to South America,' I wrote. 'Lots of love, Joe.' I handed it back to the lady who had now taken over the office.

'Have you got your instruction?' she asked in a motherly tone.

'Yes,' I said.

'Let me see it, son.' I handed over my telegram, which I had read a dozen times and folded neatly into four. 'You can catch a bus across the park, a No. 9. It will drop you at the dock gate.' She handed it back, much to my relief: its very possession filled me with strength and confidence.

The double-decker green bus finally came and, stowing my case under the stairs, I sat in the seats that faced each other across the aisle. The initial interest my fellow passengers showed in me soon reverted to boredom, and I felt sorry for them as they headed towards another miserable day the same as the last, while I was joining a ship bound for foreign places. My secret warmed me as I looked more closely at the faces opposite. They weren't just vacant; they were avoiding me. Of course they had seen my case, and could guess that I was going to the docks. This was undermining their featureless lives. Wow! I was getting arrogant to make such assumptions – but maybe just a little cockiness was allowed today. After all, it was rather special: it wasn't every day one set off on such an adventure.

The bus duly deposited me at the dock gatehouse, where I showed my instruction telegram. 'She is on number five. Follow the road round,' barked the old man, not even removing the cigarette from his mouth. He slammed shut his little window.

I looked at the road – but should I go to the right or left? – The right. Okay! My tummy was full of butterflies; shortly I would catch sight of it, its gleaming white hull the most elegant of sights – I knew it would be. On either side, large grey sheds seemed to go on forever. Tall black cranes stood in lines alongside them like sentinels, working cargoes, of ships that seemed to lean drunkenly against the wharfs. Gulls screamed aloft in the grey, overcast sky, as if claiming that this was their world, while others sat atop the sheds and watched my progress in disinterested silence. This was heaven. Yet not quite perfect: my case seemed to be getting heavier, the twine now cutting red weal's into my hands. If only it had a proper handle. I now had to swap hands every 50 yards. I had been walking for over an hour, and still no white liner, when some wharfies asked what ship I was looking for. 'The Princess Tara," I told them.

'Oh, you're almost there. You'll see it when you get to the end of shed twelve.' They all laughed.

'Thank you,' I said gratefully.

With renewed energy I gathered pace. Only another 500 yards or so to go. I rounded the last shed and there sure enough sat the Princess Tara – but could this be right? She was an old, black-hulled cargo boat, and between where I stood and the ship was a hundred yards of inky black water! Slowly the bitter truth dawned. I had come the wrong way – I should have turned left at the gate. No wonder those wharfies had such a good laugh, and were still laughing when, embarrassed, I had to pass them again on my way back. Even the gulls flapped their wings and screeched. In my embarrassment I imagined they knew too.

Almost two hours after arriving at the dock gate, I finally stood at the bottom of the gangway, my hands now bleeding from the twine. My whole body ached from toiling with the suitcase. My white liner turned out to be a 7000-ton pile of rust. Yet my heart was still excited. I dragged the case up the step rope-sided gangway and heaved it over the scupper on to the deck. The hard iron surface of which, greeted my knees with swift rebuke as I stumbled aboard. The deck, superstructure, and machinery were all painted a sickly buff colour, not an inch of gleaming white anywhere. Rust was apparent on all surfaces, the many coats doing little to hide its rampant damage.

Two men walked across the foredeck to where I had collapsed in a pile with my case.

'Who the hell are you?' demanded the young one.

'I am the new steward,' I replied, struggling to my feet. My navy blue serge uniform, emblazoned with badges, should have made that clear. The need to ask was not, I realised, to get an answer, but to establish authority from the first moment.

'You'd better come with us,' the authoritative one snapped, turning to lead the way into the amidships accommodation.

I found myself in a cabin with two bunks on one side, a settee under the porthole and another bunk on the other side. Three narrow lockers stood near the door. All of this would have been fine but for the five seamen in the cabin already. An air of expectancy was heavy in the air, as was the smoke, for it seemed they all smoked.

'This is Stretch,' said the bully who'd met me on deck,

introducing a tall, gangling man who, it transpired, was the assistant cook, 'and this is what you will get if you disobey my orders.' Stretch's trousers dropped around his ankles; briefs too, as though on cue. What I saw was his huge, flaccid penis, a tool any self-respecting donkey might be proud of. 'And I am the Second Steward – your boss, and you do what you are told, or you get some of that'.

'Yes, sir,' I squeaked quietly. They all laughed, and then set about stripping me naked. Fear now gripped my heart; my remaining strength drained from me; I felt helpless. Engine grease appeared from nowhere and they covered me with that and black shoe polish. My panic subsided as I realised that Stretch was not to be my fate – not this time. This initiation ceremony was normal it seemed, yet I was quickly realising life at sea was not going to be at all like I'd imagined!

The second steward, who obviously found considerable pleasure in such occasions, stood up. His eyes seemed somehow different; they were upside-down – straight across the top and curved around below. 'Remember, you are not a steward. You are a cabin boy and your uniform, which you won't need, is at the masthead.' They all laughed and exchanged lewd comments about me.

I was left alone, surveying the damage, when the door opened and in came a boy with whom I discovered I was to share the cabin.

'It's bloody awful to get that stuff off; I joined last Friday and got the same treatment. It was three days before I could get rid of most of it.'

'Did you get the Stretch threat as well?' I asked.

'Oh yes, but I shouldn't worry too much. All new ratings get the same treatment. My name is Billy. I'm the galley boy.'

'Where are you from?' I asked.

'Stepney,' Billy replied, with a matter-of-fact air that seemed to imply a street-smartness which his cockney accent reinforced.

'What about the second steward? He seems to be a bully.' I pictured his thick neck and cruel mouth.

'Yes, you'll have to watch out there,' Billy replied, as though knowing some secret he was not about to reveal.

I realised Billy was much more used to the rough stuff than I was, and if he was scared of the 'Second', I'd do well to keep out of his way – but how could I do that on a boat?

However, I liked Billy. I felt he was straightforward and I was sure he would be up with the play, able to advise me on how to avoid some of the pitfalls of life at sea.

'By the way," Billy asked, 'What's your name?'

'Joe,' I said tentatively, offering my greasy hand before pulling it back. 'Sorry.'

'They won't call you Joe, it'll be "Cabin" – cos they don't call me Billy – it's Galley, because I'm the galley boy, and this is my bunk. Yours is the top one – okay?'

'Yes, that's fine,' I replied, having learnt already at the Vindi that the top, although more difficult to make up and get in and out of, had some advantages: it was fractionally more private, people didn't sit on it with their bare backsides, and it also had an element of safety. 'So who sleeps there?' I asked, pointing to the bunk on the opposite wall.

'Oh that's Rose's. Take my advice – don't sit on it,' said Billy with a smile.

'Can you show me where to go for a shower? I've got to get this stuff off me before I can get dressed!' I asked.

'Oh yes, of course. I'm sorry mate. C'mon, grab your towel and follow me.' We ducked across the alleyway into the latrines. There were four showers, a urinal and four toilets.

'Oh, thanks, Billy. I'll see how much I can get off.'

'Here. You need this,' Billy said, handing me a large scrubbing brush and a square block of hard, yellow soap.

'The grease isn't too bad.' said Billy, 'but the boot polish is really hard to get out. Here. I'll give you a hand with your back.'

I thought about that for a moment. 'Okay. Thanks, Billy.'

'You'd better get used to calling me Galley,' he said, as he started taking a layer of skin off my back.

'Hey, hey, go easy!' I complained. 'All the bits will fall out if you take any more skin off.'

'It's okay, I'll leave you to it. See if you can do better on your

14

front. I'll ask Rose to come and do your cock if you like!' he said, drying his hands.

'Don't you dare. I can do it myself!', but looking down at all the black grease I realised it was going to be a long scrub.

An hour later I still looked as though I'd just come up from the pit, but at least the grease was gone and I could put some clothes on. I tried to untie the knotted string holding my suitcase together, finally gave up and used a knife to cut the bonds. I found my jeans and a fresh white shirt, looking in the mirror; I thought I looked like Al Jolson with a crew cut!

I stowed my gear and hid my diary in the canvas mattress cover. My mum had made me agree to keep the diary every day as a condition of allowing me to go to sea. She said it helped to remember the truth, not what the years turned it into. I honestly didn't understand that, but I agreed. I would have agreed to anything, let's face it. Yet already I could see a problem. There were going to be things either I couldn't write about or I could never let her see.

* * *

CHAPTER 2
Ship's Routine

Life on board quickly became highly organised, and as had been made so resoundingly clear to me on my first day, the best way to stay healthy was to keep my mouth shut and do as I was told. Cheek from one of such lowly station as I, would definitely not be tolerated. With the passing days I looked less and less like a pit boy, as the dye from the shoe polish treatment gradually leached away.

The second steward was to be, I soon discovered, not only the issuer of all instruction and task provider, but also the cause of much fear and dread. He was not as tall as Stretch at 6'6" or the cook, who was 6'0", but to me he seemed threatening all the time and therefore his presence was imposing. In actual fact he would not have been more than 5'8", but from my height of 5'4" he appeared large. He always wore his sleeves rolled up high to show off his muscles and his tattoos. When he spoke to me it was either an order or an insult. At other times he was forever relating his successes with various women or how drunk he had been on some occasion. His thin, cruel mouth wore a permanent sneer. I couldn't understand why he valued such outrageous behaviour so highly – 'And after I'd screwed her, I chucked up all down her,' he would say. 'You should've seen her face.' His upside-down eyes would glint with remembered excitement. His heavy Liverpool accent demanded concentration, for to ask him to repeat an instruction, I soon learned, was to be avoided.

My daily routine started at 6.30am, scrubbing the starboard alleyway, which ran the length of the main accommodation mid-ships, before serving breakfast to the ship's officers, of whom there were eleven. The rest of the day was spent cleaning, scrubbing, polishing and serving more meals, through till about ten at night. However, during the afternoon we enjoyed a rest. This period was aptly termed a 'make and mend', giving one the opportunity to wash, iron or sew, where necessary. Needless to say, most slept! At least, at sea we did. If we were in port, other matters took precedence.

After three days of taking on stores, it was finally time to sail from Hull: the most exciting event of my life. During the war we had been bombed continually, and as a result had moved from place to place, but nothing came close to the thrill of seeing those lines taken up. Slowly the two tugs pulled us away from the wharf, one with a line to our bow, the other astern, correcting the drift caused by the strong current. The churning brown waters swirled to the efforts of the tugs. The fine drizzle lent a misty, magical air to the scene, our black hull standing high in the water, for as yet our cargo of cement was not on board. The gulls screeched overhead, as though they had been carefully orchestrated to farewell us. Even our ugly buff superstructure and not being a streamlined, white liner, at that moment just didn't seem to matter anymore. I was proud of the ship, as perhaps only a fifteen-year-old first tripper could be.

The factories and dock buildings started to slip behind us as we nosed our way out to the waiting North Sea. Finally the tugs reclaimed their lines and we were free. The cold biting wind and rain were as welcome friends, to be savoured; I could taste the salt on my lips and smiled contentedly. This was the beginning of the adventure, and for that moment my life was perfect. Under my feet I could feel the throb of the engines as we gained speed out into the grey, horizonless North Sea. I wondered how long before we lost sight of the land, and were really at sea.

'Suppose yer think yer on yer Daddy's yacht,' growled the Second, in my ear. I spun round to see his big, leering face close to mind.

'No, Second,' I spluttered.

'Then get inside and get the pantry "boxed off"'. He grabbed my ear and led me wincing through the hatchway.

'If you want to act like some bloody passenger then do it in your off-duty time, not when you're supposed to be working,' his beery breath following me into the pantry.

'Get these dishes strapped up then mop out, before the skipper's round at ten.' Before me the pantry was full of the dirty plates and dishes from the saloon.

The following morning we were heading inland again, up the River Thames to Gravesend, to take on our cargo of 7000 tons of cement. The estuary was busy with ships setting off for distant shores. Mainly cargo vessels, laden with machinery and products, they would no doubt return with fruits from the tropics and lamb from New Zealand. Then my eyes caught sight of a liner. It was huge, it's yellow hull filled with row after row of portholes, its decks still full of passengers eager to not miss their last sight of Blighty. The murky brown and silver water gave little reflection of the passing elegance. Her stern must have shown at least four decks; under the lowest were the words 'Orcades London'. As she glided past us without a sound, a few passengers waved down to us. I wondered what they thought of us, certainly the lady and the tramp. One day, I thought, I would get a on a big liner like that.

Four days later, fully loaded with cement and sitting much lower in the water, we once more steamed out into the North Sea, where the green waves now seemed much bigger, their tops being whipped off in the brisk wind that had come up. Turning to starboard our bow now punched directly into the wind and sea. It was very cold and wet on deck, so I stepped back inside, the warmth enveloping me. It was afternoon rest time and it seemed all other hands already had their heads down, so with a cup of tea I returned to my cabin.

'The Second been giving you a hard time again, Cabin?' said Billy.

'Oh, he caught me out on deck as we were coming up to our berth. Why can't people call me Joe?'

'Dunno. It's just tradition, I told you before. Galley is just as bad. You'll get used to it.'

'I think it saves them having to remember our names,' I observed.

'Are you two going to gossip all afternoon?' snapped Rose.

I pulled myself up into the top bunk, my one refuge, my own space, and lay on my back looking past my feet. A little to the right the porthole framed the sea outside as it dashed past. We had started to roll a little and the sea outside disappeared from view to be replaced with the grey heavy sky, which was, for that moment, all the world outside. Not for long, though, for as quickly as it had gone, the grey-green sea filled up the porthole again. My fascination with this constant movement soon ebbed when I became aware of a slightly unwell feeling in my tummy. I closed my eyes to shut out the sight. In the silence that followed, I lay quietly sorting out how my new mates stood.

Though at that stage I didn't fully grasp why the steward was called Rose, he (or rather she) was higher in the pecking order than either of us and, to be honest, was the only senior who spoke to either of us pleasantly. I had actually overheard her telling off the Second for always yelling at me, so she was the nearest I had to a friend on board, besides Galley of course. For some reason they didn't seem to pick on him quite so much. I'd asked him why the Cook and his assistant didn't bully him.

'Oh, they tried, and the Cook is a real smartarse, but he knows better than to get funny with me.' Billy had an air of confidence about him, his East End upbringing serving him well, and though he was not a year older than I, he seemed so much more worldly.

* * *

19

CHAPTER 3

A Backward Glance

As my eyes closed, I saw my mother at the back door, waving me off with a reminder not to speak to strange men. I wondered what she would make of the crew of the good ship Princess Tara: of those I'd met, 'strange' would be one of the milder adjectives. Yet my mother's life had not been what could be described as normal.

She had come from a family of miners and mill workers, her thirteen brothers and sisters all following the accepted lifestyle into which fate had placed them. The men went down the pit; the girls to the mill, a large dominating building in the next street. The girls, of course, dreamt of only one thing: getting married and having their own family. This, considering the hardship that coloured their lives, might seem strange, yet they knew no alternative. It was considered normal. Those who stepped outside the bounds were the subject of much criticism. This was then, only to be expected in mum's case, for she went on the stage with the Jackson Girls, and danced her way across Europe and America. It would be reasonable to assume that she had met her fair share of strange men.

However, 'don't speak to them' on a ship would be not only difficult but unwise. I was going to have to not only speak, but live with them. Yet, from experiences to date, it was not the Roses of this world who seemed a problem – in fact quite the contrary: before coming to sea, I had spent a year working at the Granby Hotel in Harrogate, where several of the waiters were gay. They had never posed any threat to me; rather, they had made it their business to see that others did not take too much advantage of me. If anything, I had not been in any danger, in so far as they each seemed to want to play the mother role, and some jealousies rose to the surface from time to time.

From 1939 to 1945 the war-time bombing of London resulted in thousands of kids being moved to other cities where the danger was thought to be less. My mother had the foresight to put me under the stairs before going to the pub. When our house was hit, I suffered little damage, or little that I now recall in detail, except the noise. The war for children was interesting: going down to the underground at night, singing much of the time, lots of fire engines, bells and sirens, and, best of all, spotting the German planes in the searchlights before being dragged off down the tube again.

After our house was hit, I was sent to Wales as an evacuee. We were still bombed, though now it was more from the doodlebugs. They were more fun, because when the engine cut out you could usually count up to twenty-one before they reached their target. They were nevertheless destructive: one night we came out of the shelter to find the house next door had been flattened. Evacuees from London were not too welcome in Wales, though. Given that we were not really housed by choice and the little food the extra ration book afforded was hardly an incentive, the resentment was understandable.

However in the end it became intolerable. I was removed, being sent to Nottingham in the Midlands, my mother's home town, the theory being that I could stay with my mother's family since there were so many of them. The reality, however, was a little different. I should explain that mum was away all the time in the Women's Royal Air Force and my father was missing (absent might be a better term). So really I was alone, and perhaps for that reason, seemed to get shunted from one relative to the next, usually after about two weeks. I don't think I was unduly terrible; just a burden in those hard days of rationing.

By the end of the war I was eight, and when mum was demobbed from the Air Force. We moved to West Bridgeford, known locally as 'Bread and Lard Island', denoting big houses and no food. Mum's job was as housekeeper to an elderly lady and her son, a painter and decorator in his late fifties. The pair of them were hideous and on several occasions threw us out. I hoped we wouldn't go back, but the reality of those times was that there were lots of widowed mothers with young children and not enough men to go round. So, like it or not, I was there at least until I could leave school, which, because of when my birthday fell, was when I was fourteen. This was not uncommon in 1952, and since my grading at school was usually forty-eight out of a class of fifty-three, it was felt I might learn more elsewhere.

It was agreed then, that it was time that I earned my keep, and to this end my working life began as a 'page boy' at the Granby

Hotel in Harrogate, little more than a hundred miles from home. Life improved immediately, except that on my second night some drunken man tried to get into bed with me, and in his enthusiasm knocked out my two front teeth with his knee. It wasn't a sexual approach; simply that I had been put in his bed and he had been moved elsewhere, though either he had forgotten, or no one had told him, which was his story. He did agree to pay the cost of the dentures though.

I later became a Comis Waiter, and eventually attended the infamous Vindicatrix sea training school in Sharpness.

Now here I was at sea, and very shortly due to 'turn to', since I had to prepare afternoon tea in the saloon. This was one duty I quite enjoyed, since the entire crew were asleep, with the exception of the duty officers. There was no one to bully me; just me in charge.

* * *

CHAPTER 4

The North Atlantic

By 4pm I had completed the afternoon tea, and strapped up the dishes, when Rueben, the cook, appeared at the doorway.

'Any sarnies and tabnabs left, Cabin?' he asked, his tone clearly saying he knew there would be.

'Yes, sir.' I passed him the metal tray of uneaten cakes and sandwiches.

'Well, would you like to bring me a pot of tea for two to my cabin in five minutes?' With that he backed out into the alleyway and headed aft to the galley.

As I prepared his tray I wondered why he was called 'the cook' and not 'the chef' as in hotels ashore, and concluded that had we been on a liner they would have addressed him as Chef, but then, perhaps he wasn't qualified for a big ship's galley and would find himself taking orders rather than giving them. He was a big man, at least six foot tall. His white jacket was never done up – it probably wouldn't meet around his ample girth – and his blue and white check trousers never quite reached his ankles. But for all his imposing size and presence, he was never without a smile, his raucous laugh in sharp contrast to Stretch's gaunt, haunted look.

I knocked on the cook's door with my free hand and it opened immediately.

'Come in, come in; just down there will be fine,' he almost whispered. This was the first time I'd seen his cabin, which he had all to himself. His bunk ran fore to aft under the port, with a small settee to the right and a chest of drawers along the other side. He even had a coffee table! It was piled high with glossy magazines, which he scooped up now to make room for the tray.

'Here. Sit down and join me for some tea and tabnabs! You might like to look at some magazines.'

He poured the tea and I eagerly inspected the magazines. They were mostly American, very large and in full colour. What was interesting were the advertisements for cars. They were two-tone, and very long and stylish, in sharp contrast to England where all cars were black.

'Have you been to America?' I asked.

'Yes, of course, and driven cars like that,' he replied. 'Drink your tea.' He looked over my shoulder at the magazine.

'Can I borrow one of these?' I ventured, feeling his ample presence now very close on the little settee.

'Oh no, but you can come and visit in the afternoons if you like. In fact, I want you to do my dhobiing and in return you can have me as a friend to visit and talk to in the afternoon. I think you might need one.'

'When am I supposed to do it? The Second doesn't let up for a minute. If he found me doing yours, he'd want his done as well.'

'You can turn to at 5.30am instead of 6.30. I will arrange a call for you,' he said, in such a way that clearly he expected no opposition to the suggestion. I was not about to argue. Not only was he senior crew, clearly giving me an order, but he'd identified my real need, for some degree of protection from the Second. I wasn't thrilled at the earlier rise, but I felt the dhobiing was well worth it.

'Here you are then, better give you something to start with.' So saying, he dumped a pile of his whites and pants in my lap. Their greasy smell wafted up. Afternoon tea was clearly over, so I made my way back to my cabin and the snores of my two cabin mates.

The following morning my early 'turn to' was not to a world of sunshine and blue skies. It was still dark, with heavy rain showing in the light from the hatchway, the seas now much heavier. One of the 'donkey greasers', a very dark-skinned Indian with a wiry build, red singlet and grimly jeans, was sitting on the hatch behind the galley sheltering from the wind and rain. He drew on his hand-rolled cigarette, looked up and asked, 'How are you enjoying your first trip? You're the cabin boy, aren't you?' I was taken aback by his Birmingham accent.

'Oh yes, it's great,' I found myself saying, not sure my brain was connected, but grateful for his friendliness.

'We're out into the Atlantic now and heading down to the

Azores; should be about four days I think.' His eyes twinkled out from his black shinning face. 'Well, it's time I got below again. He shuffled away, disappearing through the hatch, which was the main engine room access. Pulling it closed behind him, shutting in the noise of the engine room.

On the opposite side of the alleyway from the galley was the laundry – a small room with two large sinks, four taps and two washboards, complete with scrubbing brushes and the seemingly endless bars of yellow soap. So I set to work scrubbing the cook's whites, trying to get the grease and stains out; by 6.30 I still had two pairs of pants to do – they would have to wait until tomorrow. It was time to start work, and reporting late was not recommended. Galley did not have to report to the Second. Although he scrubbed the port side alley, he took orders from the cook.

'Where the hell have you been? You're late,' the Second growled as I entered the pantry (his headquarters).

'Playing with your plonker, I bet. Well, grab this.' He thrust the large galvanised bucket at me, scrubbing brush and soap already in it, and the prickly pad for kneeling on.

The alleyway, which was about 50ft long, was an easy task in port, but at sea it was a totally different challenge. Starting from the after end outside the galley, I would work my way forward on my knees, filling the scrubbing brush with yellow soap, briskly scrubbing all I could reach before rinsing the brush and scrubbing again, finally wiping away the soap with the cloth. This sounds easy, yet in the North Atlantic Ocean it is anything but. As the bow of the ship pitches down into the trough of a big sea, the steel bucket goes racing off some twenty or twenty-five feet ahead, the soapy water making its drunken skate both swift and almost silent. As the bow comes up again to rise above the next wave, the bucket races back – not in a straight line, for the ship is rolling heavily – but snaking down the alley, spilling soapy water as it goes. My task was to keep out of its way as it hurtled past and to rinse my cloth or brush as it swept by. On the few occasions that I did get in its way, I found it could easily take a chunk out of my arm as it passed or, especially when it was coming from behind, it would empty the entire contents up my back. So very quickly the battle lines were drawn: I could not afford to let it win! I had to have the task completed, myself washed and brushed to report to the pantry for 7am to serve breakfast.

By 9.30am I was definitely having doubts about a career at sea.

I felt awful. I had already lost my breakfast and everything appeared green – including me. My world took on a surrealistic quality and I felt I was definitely going to die. Seasickness was not just feeling unwell; it was a complete mental fatigue and frustration at everything always moving. I asked the Second if I could collapse in my bunk, as the two officer cadets had been allowed to. His face positively lit up.

'Lie down, don't feel very well. Would you like mummy to come and tuck you up? Oh, I've got just the thing for you! Make you feel like a new man,' with which he burst out laughing. I could not appreciate his humour. Reaching into his locker, he produced a tin of Brasso and two cloths. 'Here you are, Cabin, come with me!'

As he led the way up on to the officers' deck and out through the starboard hatch, the wind forced us to grasp the rail to go forward, and he shouted to me to get these ports cleaned and enjoy the fresh air – 'make you feel better in no time'. I looked at the row of brass-rimmed portholes encrusted with green, salted edges, then hopefully at the Second. Clearly I had already brightened his day quite enough. I would not give him the satisfaction of my begging. He reminded me of Stretch and said that if he found me inside before he gave permission, this afternoon would be 'fun for all'.

So I set to work. I had nothing left to be sick with and it was bitterly cold up there; the only thing I could do was work and generate some body heat. With my knife I was able to scrape off most of the calcified salt and then the Brasso worked well. The only thing I didn't like was that every time the ship pitched forward very heavily – about every seventh wave – the bow dug in and the angry green water burst over the decks, the spray from which pinned me to the bulkhead with an icy force that knocked the breath out of me. This forced me to use one hand to hold the rail all the time. I was kept out for only two hours, yet it felt like a lifetime. I'd lost all sense of feeling in my hands and had been drenched continually. I was vaguely aware of Rose's face in the porthole I was polishing. The next thing I knew, she was outside on the deck and, with a surprisingly strong arm, dragged me back through the hatch and down to our cabin. In no time she had my wet clothes off, dried me down and put me in dry clothes. Galley had brought me a mug of tea; he said nothing. Rose, who was always quiet, was now obviously angry, muttering about 'that bastard'. This surprised me and made a considerable impact, for I had never heard Rose swear. That she did now made her anger the more impressive. I wanted to calm her down.

'He said it would cure my seasickness, and it has helped,' I said, not knowing why I should defend the Second's actions.

'If he wanted to be so cruel at least he could have given you a safety harness. He's crazy; he needs his head read. There are forty foot bloody waves out there and this old tramp's rolling like a bitch. He wants locking up. I'd love to get him out there for two hours – see how he'd like it.'

'I am all right, Rose – honest, come on, we'd better get set up for lunch or I'll be in trouble again. Please don't say anything Rose,' I pleaded.

'Huh. Bastard,' was all she said. Pulling on her immaculate white jacket, she wet her finger in her mouth and smoothed her eyebrows, leaving me to grab my blue and white jacket and hurry along behind her into the pantry. It seemed natural that everyone called her Rose and referred to her as she, as though at sea there were different rules and values.

The Second was waiting, his hands on his hips, grinning with his cruel lips. 'Still feel seasick, Cabin?' he jeered. I didn't answer, but ducked past him, grabbing the tablecloths for the saloon, and though: even if the Second's a real man, I feel Rose is much more respectable, more refined. I don't care if she is homosexual. I wondered how my cousins ashore might view Rose. Respectable would not be their choice of word. Yet I did respect her, probably more than anyone else on board, though of course I would not say so out loud. Perhaps we needn't blindly accept those values society put on us; maybe they were meant just to get us safely started! Wow – that was quite exciting, though what about the responsibility that came with it? Too much for me – I would need to take pretty small steps.

'Rose, may I ask you a question?'

'Yes, but work and talk at the same time. You've no time to dream with those knives and forks. C'mon.'

I continued laying up the places. 'Well, I was just wondering how you know what's right and wrong. I mean, your life is different from the rest of ours.'

'Well, actually it's not that different, Cabin. You'd be surprised. I mean, sure I don't fancy women sexually – nor little cabin boys!

27

There are men who hate women and like young boys, and often they are the ones you'd least suspect – usually married. So you must learn not to take things at face value. But as to how you know what's right and wrong, you just do. Not always thinking, but feeling. You know – if in doubt, ask yourself if you would like someone to treat you that way, or do such-and-such. You always know, since you've got to be honest to yourself, not smart, not bigger than anyone else, not even fitting in with their rules; just be straight with yourself. Now, enough, get those glasses polished and the cruets topped up.'

The saloon was soon set up for lunch, with wine glasses twinkling as the ship's movement kept changing the light. The rich, wood-panelled bulkheads imbued the atmosphere with security and comparative luxury. The new queen's portrait hung above the diners. Rose commented she wasn't sure two queens in one saloon as a good idea! She preferred Georgie. I was to learn that this was just talk: Rose was a staunch royalist, well read on the subject, and woe betide any detractors. There were a few of them amongst the crew; however, they soon learned to keep their mouths shut in front of Rose, who knew even the dogs' names.

* * *

CHAPTER 5

Sea Male

We spent the next five days sailing over the heaving, grey-green mountains of the North Atlantic. The driving wind pulled the crests off the tops of the waves, creating a skin-stinging bite for those who found themselves on deck. Each morning after breakfast, my two hours cure for seasickness was the same – polishing the brass portholes on the deck below the bridge. The seven heavy brass rims were the same each day. I had hoped for some gradual improvement, but no, they always presented the same lumpy, green, salt-encrusted mess as before. I longingly searched the sky for some blue in the clouds; some sunshine would be very welcome. But the heavy clouds came right down to the sea, with not a speck of blue to be seen, nor any land, or even other ships. Visibility was poor – a couple of miles, no more – and the only other life was the huge black-blacked gulls riding the troughs between the waves. I enjoyed watching them, for their wings didn't need to flap; the strong wind gave them power to skim inches above the sea, racing up the back of a wave then soaring high above to remain seemingly suspended. The only thing to move was their head – to spot a likely target 200 feet below and dive again, awkwardly down like a broken doll, wings half in, into another forty foot –ice-cold grey-black canyon, pulling out of the dive at the last second to cruise again just above the angry froth of the waves. How, I wondered, in all this powerful ocean, could they know always which waves would not engulf them into oblivion?

Now that I had a safety harness clamped on to the rail, thanks to Rose, I could take more enjoyment from the fresh air cure, instead of the fear of the first day. One morning, the ship, coming out of a deep pitch, rolled over drunkenly to starboard. The wave that had broken over the bow rushing down the starboard deck, completely engulfing the rail. My tin of Brasso slipped out of my hand as I clung to the tie rail. It shot off the deck and into the passing wave, and was gone so quickly, so finally, I was glad of the harness: if that had been me, no one would have seen it happen and I would have had no chance of surviving. I must thank Rose!

After lunch I was glad to crash in my bunk; the increasing rolling and pitching was exhausting and made every task harder. I was no longer vomiting and the spinning in my head was easing, but I was still drained. The reality of actually being at sea was far from my romantic dreams. So many things, so simple on land, were extraordinarily difficult at sea. Washing my face was a trial. The water in the basin would fly up to soak me or dash off to one side – anything but stay in the sink. Even the soap wouldn't stay still. A slow trickle of water from the tap was the only answer, and that required unusually dexterity. The galley was perhaps the worst place to be in such a relentless sea. I poked my head around the corner one morning, to collect the breakfast bins to take up to the saloon. Stretch had just broken a couple of eggs into the big, black frying pan. No sooner had they started to take form, than they flew out of the pan and hit the bulkhead. The cook, whose ample form was safely wedged between the doorjamb and the bench, reached into the large bin full of eggs and took out a big handful, which he then brought down on top of my head.

'There you are, Cabin. We can't cook them it seems today. Stretch has decided to decorate the bloody bulkhead with them, so you'd better have some.' With that he squashed them over my head, laughing heartily 'Great for the hair!'

The sticky yellow mess covering my face dripped down on my shirt. I ducked across to the laundry, ran the cold tap into the huge sink and struck my head under the running water. As I bent over with my head in the sink trying to rinse out all the egg slime, I felt Rueben's weight press against me.

'You can tell those topside ponces it's "hard tack" today. The galley is closed,' he whispered in my year, 'and I'll see you at two o'clock!'

Back in the pantry I reported the cook's message to the Second. To my surprise he accepted it with a smile, and turning to Rose he said, 'You'd better let them know in there, it's toast and marmalade this morning and cornflakes if they will hold their dishes.'

'What about porridge?' countered Rose. 'Stretch always has some porridge on the go, no matter how rough it gets. I'll go and see that lovely boy!' With which she headed off down to the galley, to return triumphant within minutes.

'That strong young man will be up with a dixie full of the cook's best porridge shortly. Really, you can't expect these big men to sail this ship on a slice of toast.' She threw back her head and disappeared into the saloon to pacify the waiting officers.

In the meantime I'd been toasting a mountain of bread while the Second cut the edges and racked it. I passed the toast and bowls of jam through the hatch to Rose. In the saloon the tablecloths were dampened down and the 'fiddles' were up, to help prevent plates and anything else going adrift. Certainly eating food was a lot easier than trying to cook it under these conditions. Cutlery was handed out with the plate of food; all glasses were stowed and heavy pewter mugs did for tea, coffee or beer.

The chief engineer was discussing the storm with the first officer. 'The bloody prop's out of the water as much as in it,' he complained 'and it's overheating the shaft and bearings.'

'Don't worry, Chief, we're almost out of it. Tomorrow at 3am we pass the Azores and you can do some bronzing on deck,' replied the Mate.

My eavesdropping could hardly have pleased me more and the Second, who had also heard the comment, said, 'Well, there you are, Cabin, tomorrow you can sunbathe while you wait for the helicopter".

'What helicopter?' I asked enthusiastically.

'Well, tomorrow is mail day. Once a week the Royal Mail is delivered, I suppose you expected it every day.'

'No, I didn't. In fact, I didn't know it was delivered.'

'Of course it is. Do you honestly think men would stay at sea without getting mail? The skipper needs his written instructions each week and he has to supply his ship's log. When you put the queen's stamp on a letter, Royal Mail have to deliver. All ships coming up from the Med, Africa and the East, or going out, have to pass near the Azores; that's why the helicopter's based there. Should drop ours off about 10am, but you won't get any unless this pantry is shining! Now get the saloon cleared and these dishes strapped up.'

The following morning, as soon as my feet hit the deck I knew everything was different. I looked out of the port and saw all of the waves had gone; as if by magic the sea was flat and shining silver in the early morning light; the sky, yellow-streaked up ahead contrasted with the dark grey night we were leaving astern. My excitement had me on deck as soon as I was dressed, and I went forward to stand on No. 3 hold in order to see all around. There was no land to be seen; the ship was making a gentle, lazy roll. I went back inside and got stuck into the cook's dhobi, happily looking forward to the mail.

By 10m I had the pantry cleaner than ever and was on deck with a mug of tea, awaiting the helicopter – always on the starboard side – though I would soon hear it, no matter from which direction it came. By 11 o'clock the Second was reassuring me that due to the storm they were probably running behind schedule. That afternoon I stayed on deck, still awaiting its arrival, eager not to miss it. I'd never seen a helicopter before, and a letter from Mum would be great.

By 7pm it was dark and we were serving dinner. The Second seemed more friendly than usual and answered my questions civilly, saying: 'Don't worry; they've got more important letters than yours to deliver. They'll be here tomorrow!'

The following day, I was on deck at every opportunity. I knew it had to be today. It wasn't until the next day that I learned just what a fool I'd been, when the Second could contain his happiness no longer and cracked up in fits of laughter.

'The little twit thinks the queen is going to send a helicopter way out here to deliver a letter from his mum!' I looked around in disbelief at the Second, Stretch, Galley and Rose – they knew all the time! Rose turned on the Second: 'You always carry things too far,' she said, and stormed off into the saloon.

'Ah, there, there, then. Is Cabin just a little upset?'

'No, of course not,' I insisted and went out on the deck to escape his jeering, my eyes hot and moist. I wouldn't give him the satisfaction of seeing my disappointment. Anyway, mum most likely wouldn't have written, and just think of the humiliation and disappointment if the mail had arrived with nothing for me. In the year and a half since I'd left home, she had only written twice to the hotel in Harrogate, and here we'd been out of Hull less than three weeks. So, I thought, it's good the mail didn't come. I felt better and went back in knowing he couldn't hurt me now.

That afternoon in the seclusion of my bunk, Galley and Rose snoring, I dug out my diary, whose empty pages glared up at me. So far I'd had no time or energy for writing as I had promised, so it was time to keep my promise and get into daily routine. But what could I say? We hadn't arrived anywhere yet, and to write about the crew would probably worry mum more than please her. I know, I thought, I can tell her how I feel, keep it positive and then I can use it to write letters.

The constant motion of the sea which at first made me feel awful, now I was beginning to enjoy. It's strangely comforting, and gives me a sense of going somewhere. I think of those blank bored faces on the bus and am grateful to be at sea. It's changing all the time, sometimes placid and silky, other times it's mountainous and angry, spitting salty foam to bite your eyes. The sky is the same, in a way. The tall grey columns of cumulus clouds that bring the wind and heavy seas give way to crystal clear blue days and pink and green dawns. Last night there was a dramatic blood red sunset and I was able to watch the sun sink right over the horizon as though the sea had swallowed it up.

'The other crew members are okay, except the second steward. I don't like him much. He's always saying nasty things about me and always seems angry. Billy the galley boy is my best friend. He is also a first tripper, though you wouldn't think so'. I wrote.

'Well, that's all for now.'

* * *

CHAPTER 6

The Store Room

The calmer weather meant that maintenance and repairs could be carried out, and on deck this meant an incessant chipping of the steel deck and bulkheads with a small sharp hammer to break away any rusting steel, of which we seemed to have a good supply. Red lead was then applied and later eventually painted over. This, of course, was the work of the Deck Department. However, Catering also had its chores, which I had little doubt the Second would enjoy.

'Come on Cabin, let's you and me go below.' I followed him down, deep into the bowels of the ship to just aft of the second hold, to the big fridges and the food storage. One room had rack upon rack of one-gallon cans of food and the deck was strewn with cans of jam that had come adrift in the rough weather of the past week.

'Right, you little toe-rag – get these cans up the ladder and stow them back on that top shelf.' There were about fifty cans on the deck, many badly dented. I could only manage one at a time, as I needed one hand to pull myself up the ladder.

'Come on Cabin, use both arms. I will be back in ten minutes and I expect to see them all stowed,' he demanded.

My build was, to be kind, slight, and so I had to make a separate climb for each can. To my dismay they seemed to be getting heavier with each new climb. Consequently, when the Second returned I had only half of them neatly stowed.

'We'll be here all bloody day,' the Second snarled angrily. 'I've told you: take two at a time.'

So, with one under each arm I made my way up the ladder again, this time having to lean my shoulder against the upright, using just my legs to push upwards. I was just nearing the top when the can under my left arm slipped as I automatically turned my hand to hold on. The drum fell to the ground, narrowly missing the Second.

'You did that on purpose, you little shit,' and he angrily kicked the ladder sideways, bringing the ladder, me and the remaining can down in a heap. With one hand he dragged me to my feet and buried his other fist up into my solar plexus. As I fell forward on to my knees he brought his fist back up and hit me in my face. It felt like it took my head off.

'Now get this mess cleared up by the time I get back,' he shouted as he stormed out again.

I slowly pulled myself up into a sitting position and checked to see what damage I'd incurred. It was surprisingly little: my left eye was starting to close up and my fingers hurt from landing with the can. The other bruises were from falling on the drums of jam. I righted the ladder, and one at a time I carried up the remaining drums. I was shaking uncontrollably by the time I'd finished, so I sat again on the deck and took some deep breaths – this seemed quite effective and the trembling soon stopped. I felt my strength coming back and really wanted out of that hold with its single, slowly swinging light bulb making the shadows reach out, then hide, and reach out again. I cautiously slipped into the alleyway, closing the hatch behind me. Ahead was the vertical steel ladder, but where was the Second? Desire for fresh air and freedom won, and silently I was up the ladder and across another alley and climbing up the final steps, when I heard the Second's voice coming from behind an opening door. It was as though my feet had wings. I burst out through the hatchway on to the open deck where the sweet, warm air and soft sea breeze almost denied the last hour.

I rushed into our cabin to find Rose sewing a button on her shorts. 'Good God, Cabin! You do pick up some rough trade! Don't tell me the Second's been trying it on in the fruit locker?'

'No, we were in the cold store stacking fallen jam cans," I replied, wincing at the pain in my fingers.

'You're going to have a right shiner by tomorrow,' chirped Galley, who was flat out in his bunk. 'I wouldn't let him get away with it.'

'Cabin's not a little tearaway like you, but you are going to have to learn to look after yourself a bit better, and that goes for you too, Romeo.'

'I can look after myself, thank you very much,' retorted Galley. 'I was the best fighter in our street.'

'Well, it's up to you, but I can show you how to protect yourself and – believe me – the day will come when you'll need it. Cabin needed it today!'

'But Rose, I'm too skinny to go up against the Second, and if I beat him, he'd get his revenge easily,' I reasoned.

'I'm not talking about fair fighting, but more the life or death stuff. How do you think I survive with some of the rugged men I meet? Now, you've seen me sitting silently in my bunk each day? Well, this is a meditation that I practice; I am letting all thoughts just fall away until I am clear. Because I do it every day it's easy to drop into that mental state at any time if I'm attacked, which leaves me emotionally free to attack my opponent's nervous system. It doesn't take strength at all, only speed and confidence, but first you must learn to become mindful.'

'When can we start?' I asked, knowing the need was becoming more urgent each day.

'When your wounds are healed. In the meantime you could read this,' she said handing me a book entitled 'The Mindfulness of Breathing', 'though I doubt you'll be able to read with that eye – anyway, we'll talk again.' Rose bit the thread above the button, neatly folded her shirt again and put it away.

The weather now was much warmer. We were now in our third week out of Gravesend and moving through the Sargasso Sea, which, despite the tales that Rueben the Cook wove about missing ships or ones with no crew on board, was uneventful. There was quite a bit of seaweed, which grew from the surface down, and more varieties of birds, but no pirates or ghost ships. In another four days we were due in Aruba to take on water and oil, and I looked forward now to our first landfall. Each day I plotted our position, mainly by guesswork at first, then by asking the Mate for our latitude and longitude, and drawing our progress on my chart, an old one the Mate had given me – probably because I was always asking where we were! It seemed so dreadfully slow. At times, to perceived any forward movement one had to look down the ship's side to see the water slipping by. The sea had become glassy and smooth and the heat caused a haze that made the horizon quiver. Now I was always searching for sight of land – my calculations had it that we should have seen it yesterday! But no. On the horizon the rain formed a dark trunk reaching up to the grey clouds. Galley came out on deck and joining me for our morning mug of tea. 'There's land!' he exploded, pointing to the distant rain. 'Look!'

'Where?' I asked. I couldn't see any land.

'Looks like clouds to me,' I said, wanting him to convince me.

A quarter of an hour later the mountainous coastline of Dominica was clear to see and several other crew members had come on deck to look. The Bosun, who seldom mixed with the catering side, informed us that we could see Puerto Rico on the port bow. We all clambered on to the No. 3 hatch to strain our eyes. Yes, sure enough, it was not so high, but land nevertheless. Spirits were high. The anticipation of going ashore put a smile on almost everyone's lips. There was a notice able buzz in the saloon at lunch time, as stories of previous voyages to these islands unfolded. From this distance they looked rugged and inhospitable, but the stories told of beautiful women and lots of drinking! Both would be new experiences for me.

After lunch the first officer invited me to the bridge, which was very sacred ground to me. I entered, taking considerable care not to do anything wrong, my eyes eagerly soaking up all the details. I had expected one of the officers to be driving, but a stocky deck hand stood at the wheel, his jeans and blue shirt in stark contrast to the officers' crisp white shirts and shorts. The able seaman briefly glanced at me before returning his concentration to the compass in front of him.

I'd love to do that, I thought to myself, and asked the seaman, 'Is it hard to steer?'

'Not in this weather. It's quite simple. The officer of the watch gives me a course. At the moment it's SW197 and I'm allowed two degrees either side of that.'

'That must be difficult if a large wave hits, say, the starboard bow. Wouldn't that push the bow around?' I asked.

'Yes, but in clear weather you can usually see it coming and put some wheel on to compensate. Where the skill comes in, is in the rougher weather when you can't even see the bow at night!'

I was very impressed and decided perhaps I wasn't quite ready for the steering Job.

'Thank you,' I said and thought I'd better catch up with the Mate, who was possibly plotting our course on the chart, which covered only our immediate area.

'Here you are, Cabin; this is our current position. We have just come through the Puerto Rico Trench, which is deepest part of the Atlantic Ocean at 28,232 feet. Since noon yesterday we have steamed a total of 153 nautical miles, and this morning we passed Dominica. Tomorrow we arrive in Aruba for bunkering. How are you getting on with your chart?'

'Oh quite good, but it seems so slow.'

'Well, yes. This is not a fast ship,' replied the Mate. 'But you want to gain knowledge and our slower speed will give you ample opportunity to learn. We might even talk the Bosun into letting you try your hand at the wheel.'

'Really, do you mean it?'

'We'll see, we'll see. For now let's see how much you've learned about charts and course plotting.'

For the next half hour he explained the effect of tidal streams and wind on course calculating, and encouraged me some working examples. Fortunately, we didn't get on to using the sextant on that first visit to the bridge. To be honest, I was more interested in looking at the bow from up there, and asking what all the instruments were.

I came up often in the afternoon and gradually began to understand some of the stuff, though it seemed everything I did grasp opened up heaps more to learn. One important benefit was that I was able to learn the where and when of much that was happening on board and so became less liable to be fooled by the Second. In fact, I soon found that my new source of knowledge was a tradable item, since ships are hives of rumour or 'buzzes'. To know which were true was valuable and bestowed a degree of esteem.

I was grateful to the Mate for his guidance and he seemed pleased when I actually managed to understand something he was teaching. Normally the Deck Department and Catering don't mix, but since I almost never saw the chief steward, I was happy to take advantage of the Mate's kindness, which gave me more sense of purpose to my day – and something to look forward to.

CHAPTER 7

Dominica to Aruba

It wasn't just me – the atmosphere on board had brightened considerably. Only first trippers actually expressed excitement. The more seasoned salts merely smiled more readily over a beer, absorbing the most recent landfall with as much expression of enthusiasm as a woman finding a new dress shop: outwardly she looks the same, but you know inside it's just made her day.

Galley came up to the pantry that evening with the dinner boxes for the saloon, and asked 'You going ashore in Aruba, Cabin?'

'Of course – I can't wait,' I replied.

'Well, you'd better make sure you can. The cook says as it's only a bunkering port, with less than twelve hours in, junior hands won't be allowed ashore.'

'He's pulling your leg – you know what he's like,' I replied.

'Well, you ask the Second and see,' Galley challenged. 'Anyway, where is he tonight?'

'I don't know. Rose is singing away in there laying up the tables – I think she knows where he is and isn't saying.' I asked her earlier and she just said, 'We don't need him, do we? Enjoy the break.'

'Well go and ask Rose. She'll know,' pleaded Galley.

'All right, I will.' I picked up the bread rolls and took them into the saloon.

'Hey Rose – will we be allowed ashore in Aruba?'

'Yes, of course you will. There's nothing there though, only oil rigs and a couple of bars. I don't think you'll like it particularly. Why do you ask?' Rose inquired.

'Galley reckons the cook won't let him go ashore, as it's only a bunkering port. If that's true, the Second isn't going to let me go, is he?'

'The captain is the one who says whether you go ashore or not, and would rarely stop you unless it was very dangerous. The most common reason is punishment. Has Galley not been pleasing the cook? – no, don't answer that: I hate sordid details!'

'Galley isn't like that,' I protested, 'and he can look after himself anyway!'

'Don't you be so quick to judge who's "like that" as you put it. He may be a hard case ashore, but at sea he could be quite different, and that big fat cook would be just the one to show him the delights of "the love that dare not speak its name"'.

'I don't understand, Rose. You're the only one who's "that way" on this ship and you don't trouble anyone, so how is he in danger?'

'You've a lot to learn, Cabin. Yes, I am the only homosexual on board, but that simply means I only go with men. The real danger is those who will go with whatever is available. They're the ones who take advantage of young men like Galley or yourself, and give us a bad name.'

I thought again of the homosexuals I'd worked with. Certainly none of them had caused me any concern, yet on several occasions the cook had been uncomfortably close to me.

'What about the Second, Rose. Do you think he's like that?'

'I doubt it, but I wouldn't trust him further than I could throw him. He seems to be so much in love with himself, but really his anger and sarcasm hide a lack of self-worth. Rape would be his way. Anyway, I've told you before to be careful – he's not right in the head. The reason he's not turned to this evening, I bet, is he's down aft trying to steal money off the donkey greasers with his tricky pack of cards – but he can't resist the booze and he finishes up losing. That's when you've got to watch yourself. Those men laugh at him because he thinks he's so smart, and if he loses tonight and comes back broke in the morning, he won't be able to go ashore in Aruba. So you can guess what your chances will be – that's right, slim. Now bring the soup tureen in. I can hear them coming down from the bridge deck.'

Out in the pantry, Galley held out the soup box. 'Well, what did Rose say?' he demanded.

'That you've got more chance than I have of getting ashore, by the look of it.' I took the soup and returned to the saloon.

The captain and his wife were first in tonight, followed by the chief engineer and the radio officer. Rose quickly had soup in front of each and ushered me out into the pantry. 'Since the Second is adrift tonight, you will need to bring in the food boxes – now remember to move quickly and don't clatter the dishes.'

I was delighted – this was a promotion. The hot food came up from the galley in square steel boxes which fitted into place on the 'dummy' in the saloon. A small kerosene flame flowed under the dummy to keep the food piping hot. Normally I was allowed only to clear plates, as the Second took the food into the saloon and his role was normally sacrosanct. It was strange how such a small and seemingly insignificant thing would be so important. On board everyone had their own Jobs and crossing those lines was almost unheard-of, as was not turning to for your duty! It felt like a double delight for me. My pleasure, I knew would be short lived: no way would I be allowed any gloating at the Second's expense. When he resurfaced tomorrow with his sore head and empty pocket, not to mention his shame at having been taken to the cleaners by the greasers (which appealed to my sense of humour), he was going to take out on me, since his authority gave him only two staff to bully and he knew better than to try any nonsense with Rose. He was aware (though he'd never admit it) that although he was heavily built and strong, Rose could make mincemeat out of him if he so much as touched her.

This had become apparent not long after we left England. A deckie seaman in his drunken enthusiasm had made the mistake of thinking Rose was available to all comers. He was not seen on deck for two days and his state when he did reappear, with a huge swollen nose, all purple and black, ensure Rose would be untroubled in future. Of course, he said he slipped off a ladder during the night, but no one believed him. If only the Second would try it on with Rose: I would quite enjoy that. Better still, the thought occurred to me, if the Second got off the ship, life would be pretty good.

After dinner was served and strapped up, Galley and I would often sit out on deck with a beer, watching the inky black sea slipping past us. Tonight there was a gentle swell and the only two sounds were the engine throbbing away far below us and the gentle hiss of the bow wave out here. Over the port bow the sun had already set, but the sky was still slightly orange on the horizon, briefly turning to green as I looked into the darkness above us filled with thousands of stars.

'I never realised there was so many,' I said, jumping up on the No. 3 hatch beside Galley.

'So many what?'

'Stars. Don't you think they're great? D'you think we'll ever have a space ship that visits the moon or Venus?'

'You've been reading too many "Eagles". I suppose you think Dan Dare is real!' Galley said cuttingly.

'Don't be daft, of course not. But when you look up there, don't you ever wonder how many other worlds with people on them there might be?' I reasoned.

'I'm more concerned with this lumbering old rust-bucket racing along at seven knots and whether we'll get ashore tomorrow, than wasting time with Dan Dare and the Mekon.'

'Well you've obviously read the "Eagle" or else you wouldn't know of Dan Dare. It's the best comic there is.'

'Yes, of course I used to get it, but that was when I was at school; I'm sixteen now and I've been working almost two years.'

'So have I,' I countered. 'I left when I was fourteen and a quarter and worked in hotels till I went to the Vindi before joining this old tub.'

'So how old are you now, Cabin?'

'Fifteen and a half, almost,' I replied. Those few months separating us seemed the difference between a young man and a boy.

'How come you got in so early? I had to wait till I was sixteen before going to the Vindi,' complained Galley.

'Well I'm not sure. There were several who were only fifteen in our batch, but like me they had all been away from home for over a year. The Children's Welfare interviewed me. I think they were the ones who let me join the Vindi.'

'Well,' said Galley 'this isn't getting us ashore tomorrow, is it? What are we going to do? I want to find a woman and have a few bevvies.' This was a need that had not yet surfaced for me: the graphic VD films shown at the Vindi were enough to keep such needs buried for a long time.

'Aren't you frightened of getting a dose?' I asked, somewhat in awe of his enthusiasm.

'Naw, they just fill you full of that crap at Vindi to scare you out of having a good time, 'cos they're stuck at home with ugly wives. Anyway, you just get a penicillin jab if you do cop a dose and you're okay in forty-eight hours.' I wasn't convinced and, as I didn't understand his need, was less than enthusiastic. Still, I did very much want to go ashore − and I'd like to see Galley find his fancy woman!

'I tell you what,' I suggested, 'if we're not allowed off, we could wait till lunch is strapped and they're all ashore, and quietly slip off for an hour or so. Even if it's just a walk around to explore a bit,' I reasoned. 'If you head for the bars, that's where they'll be and they'll catch you.'

'No, they won't,' retorted Galley. 'I've got it figured. One of the deckies was telling me that just past the bars there's a street where some girls hang out of their windows, so we won't have to go near the bars.'

'Okay, I'll come with you - but I don't want to go with a girl,' I said flatly. 'But there's still the Second. If he doesn't go ashore he'll make sure I don't.'

'Don't worry about him − he'll get a "sub" and be off, like a rat up a drainpipe.'

At 5.30am the following morning, before doing the cook's dhobiing, I was on deck straining to see Aruba which, much to my disappointment, was as yet no more than a small low-lying island that looked like a pencil laid flat on the horizon, the rising sun catching the yellow of the land against a still dark-grey sea and sky.

By 7.30am we were alongside − and instead of palm trees and beautiful scenery, the almost treeless island was dry and arid with oil 'donkeys' continually pumping their black gold for the ESSO Corporation. There was no town as such to be seen; the only buildings visible belonged to the port authority or oil companies.

'Haven't you got any work to do?' bellowed the Second from the open doorway.

As I turned towards him his heavy hand connected with the side of my head and sent me crashing to the deck. 'I've only just come out to see the place,' I said defensively, as I scrambled to my feet.

'Well, don't expect to be going ashore; you've seen all you're going to. Now get inside.'

His head obviously hurt more than mine and his bullying was probably meant to cover up his hangover. I slipped inside, brushed myself down and slipped quickly into the safety of the saloon, which was full of dockside officials getting stuck into their 'perks' breakfast. Most seemed to be 'customs', who certainly wouldn't find much contraband on this ship: We carried only cement. Even so they left with 'gifts' of booze and cigarettes brazenly tucked under their arms. I naively thought they must know the skipper well – or the chief steward.

It seemed strange to me that whilst I saw the captain every day. I had only ever seen the chief steward once, when I had occasion to go to his cabin to get the medical box for some ointment to treat the styes on my eyes. The air was rancid with stale cigarette smoke, but to my surprise he was fully dressed in blues, even wearing his peaked cap. He stood up from his small desk, looked at me, and without a word recovered a green mental box from the bottom of his wardrobe. He put it on his desk with a thump, then slowly undid the clasps and reached in for a tube of ointment. 'Styes is it?' he asked, and started coughing. His pale, flabby face winced with the pain of the bout.

'Yes, sir. Thank you, sir,' I said, accepting the tube. I left his cabin with speed. Once outside I gulped for air. I could still hear him coughing his heart out. I knew now why no one went in there. My swollen eyes seemed so trivial compared to that man's suffering.

Returning to our cabin I found Rose there darning a sock. 'Does the captain know he never leaves his cabin?' I asked.

'There's not much the skipper doesn't know about, believe me. However, he had a command in the North Atlantic with the chief and a U-boat sank their ship. It was five days before their lifeboat was picked up, and that's a long time in an open boat in the North Atlantic. Anyway, there's a bond between them. The skipper worries about him, and knows he won't last, but he won't put him ashore.'

'He told me that he was an alcoholic and it was best he stayed in his cabin. The only two people who ever see the chief steward are the second steward and me, and that no more than necessary. You might not think it, but he's very well read, you should see his books!' he added.

44

Well, if he's so smart why doesn't he get himself together instead of rotting away in there?' I queried.

'His wife left him for a man from the Inland Revenue, so he got screwed twice, you might say. He's been on the bottle ever since – over two years now, they say. He won't last this voyage out, you mark my words. Then your friend the Second will become the chief? How do you like that eh, Cabin?'

'Can't we do something to help?' I asked with a certain amount of enthusiasm.

I don't think so. He's very close to the skipper. If anyone could help him, the skipper would.'

Galley grabbed me at smoko. 'Is the Second letting you go ashore? Stretch told me he lost over thirty pounds last night and the game went on past three in the morning, and he's not very happy this morning: that's more than his wages for a month.

'You could say he's unhappy,' I replied. 'He said I have to stay on board.'

'But you're not going to, are you? You agreed last night to come with me.'

'It's all right for you; the cook doesn't belt you every time he's upset. He clouted me this morning just for going on deck for two minutes.'

'Well, I'm going, and if you're too chicken I'll go without you.' So saying, he went back inside, leaving me to figure out whether I preferred Galley's rejection or the Second's – after twenty-one days at sea I wanted to go with Galley, but did I have the guts?

* * *

CHAPTER 8

Aruba

At14.15, our works done, I headed for the gangway, at the head of which sat the Bosun, checking all who came on board and, more importantly, who went ashore.

'Are you not going ashore, Bosun? I asked rather cheekily, as if chatting as we went by made us invisible.

'I went ashore this morning, but you aren't going, son. Your boss said no shore leave for you, but don't worry: you're missing nothing. You too, Galley.'

'It's just I'd like to walk on the ground and be able to say I've been here after more than three weeks at sea,' I reasoned.

'Well, I'm going,' said Galley. 'The cook's been ashore since eleven o'clock. He'll be too engaged in other things by now to even recognise me.'

'He'll still know you've been ashore by checking the list. And as for you, Cabin, you'd be crazy – take my word, it's not worth it. The Second has already loosened a few of your teeth,' said the Bosun, 'Don't give him the excuse to break any more.'

I felt the weight of the Bosun's argument and said to Galley, 'You'd best to go without me.'

'Well okay, mate, I'll give her one for you – you don't know what you're missing,' and he clattered off down the gangway.

I watched Galley disappear through the dock gates and up the road to adventure. The pull to follow him was very strong. I looked at the Bosun, his eyes met mine. 'Don't even think about it,' he said quietly, but with an authority that reduced my longing to go ashore. 'You'll thank me later – and you'll get plenty of shore leave in New Zealand.'

'Go and get your head down. We sail at seven and you'll be on duty at five – and probably the only one sober in your department, so happen you'll have plenty to do.'

As it turned out the Bosun was right. I tried to sleep, but kept finding myself in turmoil, wanting to be ashore with Galley. I went on deck again about 4.30 to watch them coming back on board, but it soon became obvious that returning to the ship was not high on anyone's list of priorities. I asked when the Bosun thought they would return – 'Well, six o'clock ship's time the limit, so don't expect too many before then. And we sail at seven. You know, this ship has the reputation of being the second worst to sail on, which means the crew's not exactly a choice bunch, so if we get them all back it'll be a wonder.

Just then, as if to make a liar of him, a taxi pulled up and out stepped Rose. Immaculate as always in light white trousers, a pink silk shirt and a panama hat, she also wore a pair of dark glasses that did nothing to hide her identify. On an island predominantly inhabited by oil men, Rose would not pass unnoticed. Only she could turn climbing the gangway of twenty-six steps into an elegant entrance.

'Don't worry dear – your aunty is back safe and sound, and I am pleased to see you had the good sense to stay on board.'

'It wasn't good sense,' said the Bosun, 'He's been champing at the bit all afternoon.'

'Well, I'll see you in the saloon in fifteen minutes. Someone's got to feed the men!' She minced away to change, obviously having had more than a couple of drinks ashore.

At 5pm on the dot she reappeared in full whites. 'Come, Cabin, let's get some work done.'

I was amazed. In less than fifteen minutes she'd transformed from a gaily dressed, sweating party-goer to a stone-cold sober, efficient steward.

'How do you do that? I enquired once inside.

'I've told you, it's all in the mind! Are you still doing your meditation practice?'

'Yes, but that's different. I couldn't change like you just did.'

'Oh yes you could; give yourself time. I've been practising for over twelve years. You've only just started; just keep doing it every day. Remember, at sea – or anywhere – if you say you're going to do something, always do it. There are no excuses. At sea it's even more important because we all depend on each other. But the important thing is to build inner strength by always honouring your word – which is honouring yourself. Don't let others distract you or tempt you. When you signed ship's articles you promised to serve the Captain and officers to the best of your ability, in return for pay, food and accommodation. The better you do your job, the stronger you will grow inside your heart and head.'

'Wow, Rose! You know so much stuff! How did you learn it all?' I asked in awe.

'Being the only homosexual on board amongst all this rabble, I've got to be smarter, or I'd end up like some of my sisters – no thank you. Now go down and see if anyone's "turned to" in the galley yet.'

Stretch, gripping the horizontal bars on the oven doors with both hands for support, wore an expression of concerted effort. His eyes were unfocused and his lips were trying unsuccessfully to form words. Clearly, he was trying hard to be in charge of cooking. Galley, still in shore gear, was rushing around struggling to interpret his instructions.

'How did you make out?' I asked Galley, who was grinning from ear to ear.

'I'll tell you all about it later. Here, take these,' pushing the rolls tray into my hands. 'I'll bring the soup up.'

'It's okay, I'll come back for the soup. You look like you've got your hands full.'

'I had them full this afternoon!' he laughed as I disappeared up the alley and back to the pantry.

'Well?' demanded Rose, stepping into the pantry.

'Stretch and Galley are now there,' I replied.

'And what state is Stretch in?'

'He doesn't look very well,' I said.

I learned later from Galley that Rose had taken Stretch to his cabin and put him to bed with orders to stay there. She returned to complete the meal preparation in record time, saying to Galley, 'Now, sweet boy, if you've washed your hands since handling that floozy this afternoon, just bring the food up the pantry and we'll manage fine.'

And we did. The officers didn't notice we were short-handed; the cook, Stretch and the Second's absence went unnoticed. I was surprised, though, at Rose's willingness to cover for them and asked her why.

'Because they'll all owe me, and that means I get left alone. So, if you recall our earlier conversation, we are stronger, are we not, by their weakness.'

I didn't really understand the value of Rose's words then, for I knew the Second was the strong one. In fact, come to think of it, everyone on the ship was stronger than I was. It seemed I had to take orders from everyone who chose to give them. The lesson I had learned – many years before joining this ship – was do as you are told without answering back. My age, skill and build allowed for little else, yet I sensed the wisdom of Rose's words even if I didn't understand them at the time. I had to acknowledge that no one messed with Rose, which, for a skinny 5'7" steward who was homosexual, was remarkable – even more so given that she apparently didn't put out to anyone.

Later I ducked out on deck for a few moments to see the lights of Aruba slipping past us as we headed out into the night and the open sea. The pilot was just jumping from the rope ladder on to the deck of his launch, which had closed up to collect him. Once he was safely aboard, the powerful launch curved away, her wake of white foam glistening under our bridge spotlight. A hundred yards further on, the bridge cut the light and the launch was swallowed up by the darkness as we plodded on towards the Panama Canal.

By 9.30pm we were all strapped up and rose, Galley and I were in our cabin. 'Come on, then, wonder stud – let's have all the gory details,' I jibed.

'Well,' said Galley, pulling the top off a beer. 'As I said, I didn't go to the bars, but tried a club. It was so dark, they put me in a booth and the next thing I know this woman's got her hands on me and I couldn't see her. She said I should buy her a drink, but my eyes weren't accustomed to that much dark, so I split out of there real quick, I mean, she could have been a hundred for all I knew.'

I laughed and said, 'Seems fair to me – she didn't have to see your ugly face either – ha ha.'

'Anyway,' Galley continued, 'I carried on walking, and about two blocks further I find these three girls standing around this doorway. One of them says, "You looking for company, handsome?"'

'I bet you added the handsome,' said Rose with a smile.

Undaunted, Galley continued.

'How much?' I asked.

'Five dollars,' said the tall one who was called Francesca. She was gorgeous with long black hair in ringlets.

'How much in English money?' I asked her.

'Thirty shillings to you – just because you're pretty.'

'Huh,' said Rose.

'Well, I'd like some of that, okay,' continued galley.

She took my hand and led me to a room at the back. It was quite nice, with a big mattress on the floor and a red cloth over the lamp. We made love all afternoon. She was terrific and what she did to me! You don't know what you missed.'

'I bet she had you out within fifteen minutes. She wouldn't give you all afternoon for thirty shillings. You're dreaming,' said Rose.

'Well, it was at least an hour,' protested Galley. 'She said she loved me and is going to write to me.'

'Yes, you and every other sailor she's had! You just pray a good time was all you got,' said Rose.

'Don't be daft – if you'd seen her you'd have known she was clean; she wasn't more than eighteen.' He insisted.

Three days later Galley was 'squeezing up' and had to go to the chief steward for a penicillin injection and some tablets. This made me feel relieved that I hadn't been able to go ashore, especially when Galley described some of the pains. I would prefer to do without, even though he said, 'It's only a dose of "guns" – it's not as though it's siph – it'll be gone in a week!'

* * *

CHAPTER 9

Panama

Galley and I sat on No. 3 hatch during our morning break and watched our approach route to the Panama Canal. From here it just looked like three pencil-thin silver strips, each standing higher than the last. We were still about eight miles off, and at anchor, along with about a dozen other ships that would be in our convoy. We were due to go through at midday, but it was actually 2.30pm before we entered the first lock. It was approximately 1000 feet long and 100 feet wide, filling up in less than six minutes. This was one of the seven wonders of the world, and we didn't want to miss any of it. The work on the canal was started by Ferdinand de Lesseps in 1882. It is claimed a man died for every inch gained through this hostile isthmus, not so much from native tribes, but from the heat, malaria and yellow fever. Now, however, it was the epitome of efficiency and engineering ingenuity. Finished by the Americans, it was opened on 15 August, 1914. The first ship through the canal was the SS Ancon. I read this in the pamphlet I had scored from the pilot in the saloon.

Two railway engines on either side, called 'mules', were attached by cables to the ship fore and aft. They guided us through into the next lock and tightened their lines as we again rose on the incoming water. Finally they guided us through to the Gatun lakes, where they released the ship to proceed the fifty miles through to the Pacific side under our own steam. Leaving Cristobal, we glided across to the muddy, orange waters of the lakes and into the narrows of the channel proper, which varied in width from fifty yards to nearly a mile. In later years some of the hills were removed to give a much wider access, particularly through the 'cuts'.

After lunch we went out again and spent the whole afternoon enjoying the transit. All around, the hills were completely covered in jungle which came right down to the water's edge. The wet heat hung in the air, almost a mist. The grey sky closing in the humid, sweet smells of the jungle's undergrowth. In the narrower cuts the trees reached out to touch our decks as we passed through.

'Do you think there are crocodiles in there?' asked Galley.

'I don't know, but I wouldn't want to swim in it; there would be snakes and all sorts. As for a quiet walk ashore, all kinds of animals, spiders and snakes – no, for once I think we're in the best place,' I said, nodding at the jungle. 'Though it is exciting, isn't it? Makes a change from Arkwright St.'

'Where's Arkwright St, then?' asked Galley, only half wanting an answer.

'Oh just a main street at home,' I replied. 'So different from all this jungle.'

'Streets in East London are like a jungle in a way,' put in Galley, 'and though we don't have any Jonny Weissmuller's, we do have a few Singhs, Chongs and Patels. That run restaurants.'

'In that little lot,' I said, pointing to the dark interior between the trees, 'It's all one big restaurant and if you went plodding through it, you'd likely find yourself on the menu.'

We looked for crocodiles or tigers, but without luck. We saw a lot of birds, especially vultures, and heard many strange sounds.

That evening after dinner we sat on deck again. I had been trying to read a newspaper I'd scored from the pilot, but the air was so heavy with moisture that the limp pages stuck together. The sweat pouring off me didn't help. I gave up. I would stow it in the engine room to dry out tomorrow. The jungle closed in on both sides and at nightfall it had come alive with the sounds of an unseen audience watching us glide slowly past, their screams, whistles and croaks a conversation that emphasised our ignorance and alienation.

'I'm glad we don't have to dig our way through this little lot,' I said.

'They were mostly French convicts and natives,' replied Galley. 'I can remember it from school, but the Americans, because they completed it, get all the fees for a hundred years. Not bad, I should think, so long as you were an investor and not a digger.'

The heat had not relented with nightfall, so going through the Culebra 'cut' we retreated, exhausted, to our cabin. Though it was no cooler, at least we could get our gear off and try to sleep with just a sheet over our sweating bodies, listening to the noise of the jungle brushing past.

The following morning we were at sea again, so saw nothing of the Miraflores Locks or of Panama City. Our bows were once more ploughing ahead to that next place over the horizon.

* * *

CHAPTER 10

Is this our doctor... No!

Three days later we laid off the Galapagos Islands to deliver a doctor to the small community there. He wasn't a proper doctor in my book, because he couldn't fix a little problem that Galley and I had. He was a scientist and seemingly an important member of the study group observing the creatures on the islands. At that time I had no appreciation of the importance of their work, or the significance of these rather unattractive islands. The small launch that came out to fetch him was old and very basic. I felt somehow let down, not only because he couldn't fix our ailments, but these apparently uninteresting islands were not in line with how I imagined the blue Pacific. [I had no knowledge of their importance in helping Darwin discover Evolution]... I didn't know it then, but the longed for palm-fringed sandy white beaches were not on the menu for this trip. In fact, a lot was due to happen that I had not anticipated. Bob Hope and Dorothy Lamour's portrayals were to remain, at least for now strictly Hollywood.

However, the need for a proper doctor arose on the first morning after Panama. We finished serving breakfast and it was time for me to have mine. Rose and the Second had theirs in the saloon. I ate in the pantry with a square biscuit tin for a seat and a tray on my knees. On this morning I sat quite heavily, for it was so low, and felt a serious pain in my backside, causing me to rise up again a great deal faster than I had sat, my breakfast tray taking off into the air with a life of its own. My yell of anguish had brought Rose into the pantry to see what on earth was happening. She had me drop my pants and exclaimed 'Oh my God, that's a mosquito bite and then some. What did you do?'

'I just went to sit on my box for breakfast.'

'You mean you didn't know you had it? Didn't it hurt before? It's as big as my fist – you're going to need that lanced.'

I didn't like the sound of that and asked, 'By whom? The Chief couldn't do it.'

'Well, you've got to empty it; you can't carry on like that. Come down to the cabin and let's see what we can do.'

By this time, the Second was hanging in the saloon doorway. 'You're not skiving off leaving the pantry in this state.'

'Oh! Shut up,' said Rose – and he did.

Rose had my galvanised bucket half full of warm water, me face down on her bunk, a bottle of Dettol and some cotton wool, and went to work with her version of 'Lancing', squeezing it all out and applying Dettol like it was going out of fashion. My appreciation of her efforts was not well phrased.

'You've got to empty it every day, and don't expect me to do it. I'm not Florence Bloody Nightingale. You really need proper medical treatment, but since we can't pop along to see the doctor you must do it yourself. Use plenty of Dettol to keep germ free.'

'Thanks, Rose,' I said, getting up, still somewhat shaken.

'When did you get bitten, do you know?'

'No, not really. Sometime during the night going through the canal, my sheet must have come adrift and the porthole was open.'

'It wouldn't have happened if we'd had a mesh. Our port's the only one without one. You leave it to me, I'll see the Bosun.'

Well that was that – or so I thought. However, Galley had been bitten also – though his was on his arm. He didn't report it, thinking it was a symptom of the 'dose' he'd caught in Aruba four days earlier. Now, when we just dropped the professor doctor off, Galley's arm was all swollen up – so much so there was no longer any single swollen area. You couldn't even see the bite anymore.

It took me at least three weeks to get rid of my problem. Galley wasn't so lucky. He still had his when we arrived in New Zealand some six weeks later. By then it was like a stiff, smooth purple log, about sixteen inches in circumstances, which he was unable to bend.

Seeing the doctor disappear ashore made me feel that our well-being was not highly rated in the scale of things. It wasn't until much later that I understood the difference between his science doctorate and a medical practitioner. For now, I thought he was selfish and I had a low opinion of him. The Galapagos Islands were welcome to have him.

CHAPTER 11

The Dead Calm

For some days now we had moved in a world that was devoid of normal weather; an eerie place with no edges, no wind and a sea without waves or even a ripple. Its slick, smooth, glossy surface of silver and grey looked totally unreal. The sky showed no blue, nor even any clouds, just an almost translucent grey which gave no measure of how near it was. The sky and the sea merged, stealing the horizon and giving one the impression of having entered a silky void that stretched forever. There were no birds or fish in this place, just the growing sound of our engine, which seemed to become louder with each passing hour.

The effect on the crew after a few days was becoming unbearable as tempers became shorter and fights more frequent. I could well understand how seamen just walked off ships in such conditions, believing they saw idyllic islands and sultry maidens calling them to come. Their seemingly meaningless responsibilities would fall away like so much dross.

In reality, the drinking increased dramatically and the early morning could reveal our cabin deck covered with inert bodies, who had felt the need for young companions the previous night. Both Galley and I had occasion to recourse to the self-defence techniques Rose had taught us, which in all honesty might not have worked had the men been less drunk. Happily for us, they were blissfully unaware of this as they shuffled off the following morning, wanting to believe they had passed out honourably. These couldn't be regarded as assaults, since even if they could've got into our bunks, they were in no fit state to have achieved anything. We laughed about it and Rose, of course, teased us about bringing such low class men to our home.

The one occasion, however, that was serious occurred on our tenth day in the dead calm. Most of the crew were now at screaming level. It was just too much for the normally jovial cook. He went right off his trolley. I was returning the buns after lunch, and as I turned into the galley I bumped straight into Cook, the buns going in all directions. He grabbed me, saying, 'There's no need to throw our buns around. That's naughty and we have ways of teaching naughty boys!' He lifted me up and pushed his big hot tongue in my ear. I struggled, but got nowhere. My arms were pinned. He stumbled out of the galley, dragging me along with him. I knew what was going to happen to me. I brought my knee hard up into his groin. He doubled up and dropped me as he clutched his balls, his eyes swollen with pain and rage.

I knew I had landed myself in deep trouble and ducked into the engine room, the blast of heat stopping me on the square yard of steel balcony overlooking the engine room. The balcony, which appeared to have been made from Meccano parts, led down some steep steps and then along the length of the engine. Escape along the walkway would have been easy, except that the three great pistons rose alternately, blocking the path of the walkway as the rise came up and over. As each shining and noisy piston moved away in a close arch, the next, driving relentlessly up and down, would block the passage. It seemed the entire engine room was a cavern of huge steel shafts pounding away in a deafening cacophony of noise, around which a myriad of walkways seemed to thread, not only along the walls but also across yawning chasms of steam and heat. The handrails were hot to the touch; in fact, without gloves they were painfully hot. Gingerly, I descended into this hellish realm, my heart thumping so heavily I trembled all over. My knees felt decidedly weak. Hot, noisy engine rooms were not my territory, and had it not been for the sound behind me of the hatch door lever being swung clear. I would have dared go no further.

I turned to see the cook framed in the doorway. He had a meat cleaver in his hand. Cautiously, I ran towards the pistons, clearing the first. I waited until the second went over and moved forward into the space. There was no room for error, and I couldn't look to see if the cook was following as I made the next and final move. But now I could feel the heavy footfalls of the cook though the vibration on the catwalk and, reaching the far end, scampered down the next set of steps.

I didn't believe the cook would follow me through the pistons. I was wrong. He was almost through and I had to find some way of keeping out of his reach. I knew down at the bottom the donkey greasers would be working and thought they wouldn't let him get me, yet I was wrong again. Experience probably on their side, they vanished into unseen caverns and shadows, I knew not where. All I realised was that I was as far down as I could get and the meat cleaver was almost at the bottom of the stairway.

There had to be a way out: where had the greasers disappeared to? Running aft I found myself in a dead end, except for some rungs in the bulkhead. The vertical climb up these was the only escape, so, with no time to spare, I climbed higher and higher until I reached a cross-bridge that spanned the room directly above the pistons. I had no choice but to inch my way across. Two questions kept coming into my head. How could his bulky size keep this up and squeeze through the narrow passages? And why was nobody coming to my rescue?

In the end someone did – a little over an hour later the second mate emerged, seemingly from nowhere, and injected the cook with a sedative. He had just started to climb a ringed vertical ladder when the Mate stuck the needle into his ample backside. The Mate said he didn't think the cook even felt it, he was so much 'out of his head'. He reached the top and was halfway along the main catwalk again when his knees just seemed to buckle under him. The cleaver dropped from his hand and fell some thirty feet to the generator below, then clattered to some dark resting place in the bowels of the engine room.

As I stepped out into the alleyway it seemed everyone had crowded in, like an audience at the Coliseum. They cheered and asked how I felt. It seemed an absurd question. I suppose they just wanted to say something, but I couldn't find an answer as their faces started to go round and round, disappearing into a black silence as I fell to the deck. Within an hour I awoke in my bunk, to be told I'd passed out with dehydration and over-heating, but was fine. I was told to drink plenty of fluids for a couple of days.

The following afternoon Galley and I sat on No. 3 hatch as usual, looking at the sea, which today was full of magic. We had come out of the doldrums and once more had a sharp, clear horizon. The deep blue of the sea was full of brilliantly radiant diamonds and a warm, gentle breeze came over the bow, which softly rose and fell into the almost imperceptible swell. Flying fish skittered over the surface of the sea, only to disappear as abruptly as they appeared. The air felt clean again and the mood on board improved dramatically; apologies were freely exchanged. Galley even apologised for not coming into the engine room yesterday to help distract the cook. Of course I said, 'Oh, that's okay. You have to work with him every day. If it had been the Second chasing you, I would probably have stayed out because I know he'd get his revenge another day.'

'Yeh, but that's different. The Second is a real nutter.'

'Your Cook was yesterday,' I said firmly. 'How is he today?'

'Quiet. Not his usually smarmy self with his sarcasm and jokes. Has he said anything to you?'

'Yes. The Bosun and first officer brought him up to the pantry and had him apologise to me. I felt sorry for him, really. I know he's not normally aggressive, but still, Rose made the Second go to the galley and bring up the food for breakfast and lunch and told me to keep out of the cook's way.'

'Well, he's not said much about it – nothing to me, anyway. He was telling Stretch he didn't really remember much – that's all. It's like it didn't happen. Don't worry, by tomorrow it will be all forgotten. Cook likes you, so you've nothing to worry about,' said Galley, laying back in the hatch.

'It's his liking that worries me,' I said, looking at my hands, all blistered from the engine room rails.

'Don't worry – just forget it –The Doldrums was enough to send anyone mental and because this old tramp is so slow we were in it for ten days.'

'Well, I prefer heavy weather to that, any day. People work together like a team then, not tearing at each other's throats,' I said with conviction.

'What's interesting at sea, is that his behaviour is logged as being "caused by the doldrums". If we'd been ashore, he would've been blamed and locked up,' said Galley authoritatively.

'Yes, I suppose so...'

'You know, the Second could have helped out yesterday,' Galley said in a low tone.

'Don't be daft. He'd have been helping Cook, not me. No. To tell you the truth, I think the Second is a coward. He may knock me around, but have you ever seen him pick up on anyone bigger than me?'

'Remember how he cut all my hair off last week and tarred me!' exclaimed Galley indignantly.

'Well he did the same to me and the two apprentices! But that was the 'crossing-the-line' ceremony, and he had the help of six others and none of us knew what was coming, because they let us out one at a time into King Neptune's presence.'

'He would be the policeman, and didn't he enjoy it!' Galley added. 'There has to be a way to get our own back.'

'Well, whatever it is, forget it, 'cos I'm the one who'll cop it the next day,' I said.

'You know, I heard one of the engineers telling Stretch that the Second had bought some dope in Aruba and was using it to gamble with the donkey greasers. When he wins he takes cash, when they wins he pays in dope – they get stoned and he plays with his tricky pack of cards.'

'What sort of dope is it?' I enquired.

'I'm not sure, but apparently it's called Black Leb, which is a compressed marijuana. Anyway, whatever it is, he reckons they're laughing half the night, and your boss has won all his losses back and then some.'

'Have you ever tried it?' I asked, knowing Galley had already drank deeply of life's offerings.

'No – it's never interested me. You can get hooked on that stuff.'

'What does it do to you?' I asked.

'Makes you laugh like a bloody idiot and you just want to do nothing,' said Galley with a silly grin.

'The engineers wouldn't like that, I bet.'

Galley thought for a new moments and replied, 'I don't know, perhaps they cover for each other. What I do know is if the chief engineer knew, he'd put them ashore pronto.'

'Could the Second get into trouble for selling it to them?' I asked.

'You bet, but no one's going to tell the tales are they? You wouldn't dare, would you?'

'No,' I replied. 'I don't care what he does; it probably brightens the greasers' lives anyway.' Though I thought to myself, if the Second knew I knew, perhaps he wouldn't knock me around so much.

* * *

CHAPTER 12

Trouble on the High Seas

The blue Pacific had added warmth and colour to our daily routine during the past week and was a welcome break. Afternoons were spent sunbathing on deck and listening to Rose's portable radio on the No. 3 hatch. Rose applied a mixture of coconut oil and vinegar all over and her body was already getting quite dark. Galley and I, as well as Cook, had a somewhat different experience. We used a suntan lotion out of ship's stores which had little effect, and instead of going brown we turned into painful lobster-coloured clowns on whom clothes were suddenly a source of agony. By the third day the novelty had definitely worn off as huge blisters appeared. The need for a film star tan had lost all its charm; instead we sat on the starboard locker outside our cabin and read Hank Janson and Peter Carter Browns which we'd scored from the second engineer.

'Why don't you read something worthwhile, instead of that rubbish,' sang Rose as she went back inside with her towels, basket, radio, and a copy of "Steppenwolf" by Hermann Hesse.

'You'd have us reading bloody Shakespeare, wouldn't you?' countered Galley without looking up.

'Suit yourself,' and Rose disappeared inside.

The idyllic weather, however, was not to last. That night as I stood up in the bow facing into the oncoming wind (as I did every night in an attempt to gain a ruddy complexion like the older deck hands), I could feel the ship gradually rising higher as the swell started to build. The last traces of the sun had long gone, but there was still enough afterglow to silhouette a mountain of cumulus clouds building on the horizon, and I wondered how the Pacific had been named, because it looked like we were about to catch some dirty weather.

By the following morning we were rolling considerably; the

fiddles were up again on the saloon tables and the cloths damped down to prevent the plates and cutlery from taking off. I was pleased that this weather no longer affected me and I was able to snake my way down the alley loaded with tins without mishap. Even the early morning scrub-out had been achieved without any damage. It was almost like getting a silent award: I was a seaman now, as good as the rest, with sea legs to prove it. This, for me, was no small victory; made all the sweeter by the two officer apprentices having to retire to their bunks heaving their hearts out. So the Second had proved right: my week of roughing it at the beginning was paying dividends now, and that realisation gave me confidence. I didn't thank the Second, for he had found enjoyment at my expense, but it felt reassuring to observe that I was making progress, even if everyone else took such matters for granted.

That night Stretch was playing cards with the Second and two deckies in the saloon. Cook had refused, saying the Second wasn't to be trusted. Stretch simply said, 'if he brings his trick cards out, he knows I'll flatten him.' By 1am the game was still in full swing and the stakes had gradually risen. About a dozen of us were watching the game and although the Second had objected to 'voyeurs', the deckies felt it kept everyone honest. Stretch and one of the deckies had been steadily accumulating most of the winnings when the Second doubled up his bet four times. Stretch was like a fly walking into the spider's web – all watching knew what the outcome would be; all the money on the table was on this hand now – over £120. Finally Stretch laid down his Jack Flush.

The Second looked worried, but held Stretch's eyes – as he laid a Queen Flush and slowly allowed a triumphant glint to come into his eyes. Stretch was speechless.

'That's just about impossible,' he said at last, his voice trembling with anger and disbelief. With a dozen witnesses who'd watched every move the Second made, no one could dispute his victory.

'Thank you, gentlemen,' said the Second as he scooped up his winnings. 'That's enough to buy me three small cars!'

All present tensed, unsure whether Stretch would let him leave the room alive. He did – not before grabbing the cards, however, 'I reckon I just bought these,' he said really close up to the Second's face.

'Have it your own way,' said the Second, ducking out and

disappearing off down the alleyway to his cabin.

'Tomorrow in daylight I'm going to examine these cards under the glass they've got on the bridge. I know he pulled a fast one,' grumbled Stretch. 'He's cleaned us three out, and I'm sure he did something.'

'We were all watching him,' said Cook. 'His hands didn't leave the table. We all wanted to catch him, but I can't see how he could've cheated.'

The saloon was soon empty and I tidied the chairs, emptied the ashtrays and cleared the debris of bottles and cans. We were not supposed to use the saloon, and we were lucky not to have been caught.

Just as I was putting the cloth back, a card drifted to my feet. The draught of shaking the tablecloth must have dislodged it. It was a seven of clubs. If I took this to Stretch, he would smash the Second into submission. That thought appealed to me and raised my spirits considerably. I would see Stretch first thing in the morning.

As I lay in my bunk waiting for sleep to arrive, I joyously went over how the Second would look when Stretch had finished with him, but then it occurred to me – how cold he prove the Second had palmed it? Maybe he wouldn't need to: losing six months pay was a lot of motivation. Then I thought, what would it achieve, really? How would Rose handle it? Well, she'd keep quiet and save it for leverage when circumstances warranted it.

That's what I'd do. It would be an ace up my sleeve, but I had to tell someone or it could be said I'd invented it, and I couldn't tell Stretch. Instead I told Rose, who said I was playing a dangerous game, and that I should take it to the Captain.

'No, no,' I said, hoping the Second hadn't heard me. 'I'll find myself overboard and no mistake. No, I'll just keep quiet, put it in an envelope and ask the first mate to put it in the ship's safe.'

That is what I did. It didn't get Stretch his money back straight away, but it kept the peace and gave me a little more confidence. In the days that followed, the Second stayed clear of the galley and Stretch argued that the pack they'd played with was blue, yet the pack he'd taken to his cabin was green. I knew, of course, because the card I'd put in the ship's safe was blue: the Second must have switched the pack after the game.

The storm was building and by the third day sleep had become impossible. Our bunks were athwart ships, so when we rolled to starboard our body weight rolled us up, head into bent knees, and rolling to port, it was necessary to kick off the bulkhead and stretch out, to prevent being rolled over backwards. To some extent this could be avoided by lying on one's side, but even then it was impossible to avoid sliding up and down the bunk. Consequently, by the time I turned to I was still tired and aching from trying to hand on to the duck-board.

That afternoon I lay in my bunk on my back holding the duck-board firmly with my right hand and pressing against the bulkhead with my left to prevent roll. As we rolled to starboard the frothy, grey-green sea came rushing up, splashing across the deck and against our porthole, filling it with green-white foam; then up we would come, the horizon falling far below and the grey skies filling our view.

Suddenly there was a heaving thud and our cabin was thrust into blackness. A few moments passed before Galley's voice loudly demanded, 'What's happening? Why's it gone dark?'

'Oh stop panicking, you two. They're just putting the dead-lights down to protect the glass in the porthole.'

We heard the squeaking of the nuts being tightened and Galley flicked on his bunk light. 'I don't like that; it's like being locked in.'

'Just thank your lucky stars it's not you out there having to batten them down. You're not allowed on deck now; all outside hatches will be kept closed,' put in Rose. 'This is the time the Deck Department earn their money.'

'How long will it last, Rose?' I asked, beginning to doubt how long my new-found sea legs would hold out.

'I don't know, Cabin. This is a hurricane and it depends which way it's going. The thing I don't like is that it seems to be going the same way as us, so it could last weeks, or just a few days.

As if to confirm her words, we rose up on a big wave and poised aloft, our propellers clear of the racing water. The stern shook like a dog fresh out of the water, until we slid down the next trough and the props bit into the angry waves, driving us faster to the bottom until we crashed into the sea ahead of us. The whole ship felt as though we had hit a brick wall and anything loose suddenly took flight, colliding with a bulkhead or deck. Hundreds of tons of water crashed over the decks as we disappeared into that awesome grey mountain of water, only to find ourselves riding high on another crest again with the engine racing, the props whining in the salt-strewn air.

Again we started our crazy surf down the wave, rolling over to starboard at the same time, until again we plunged to the foot of the next wave. It felt as though the ship was totally submerged. Whether we imagined that I don't know, but we did hear the sea smashing against our porthole and knew we were underwater at least to our level.

Three more days of this hammering and a lot of damage was building up. We were running before the sea, with sea anchors out, yet when we hit the bottom of those troughs the ship took such a shock, it was losing some of the hull's rivets. We could hear them pinging off into oblivion. To say this was disconcerting would be an understatement, but to make matters worse, the sea was getting into No. 5 hold through the loosened hatch beams. The covering tarpaulin had ripped loose along one side and was thrashing angrily in the high wind. What made this even more urgent was that the water was turning the cement into concert, increasing its weight quite markedly. As the concrete swelled it prized open the ship's plates along the hull, causing yet more rivets to ping away into the deep.

This added weight of the concrete meant the stern was underwater much of the time, flooding the aft accommodation. The Bosun and his mate strung lines along the deck and, using a harness strapped around them and locked to hose lines, they rescued the twelve crew who were trapped in the flooded accommodation; gaining enormous respect for their skill and bravery.

The only way I could see out was over the after hatch porthole on the officers' accommodation alleyway above our deck. It was some relief from what I imagined was happening when I was down below and unable to see.

The stern was under water most of the time, except when we were carried on top of an enormous wave. With my nose hard up against the glass, I could see the waters draining from the decks, the poop high in the grey sky. The whole ship shuddered as the propeller raced on, biting only air. A flash of lightning momentarily lit up the angry sea; as if on cue we started down the next crest run, then bang – we hit the bottom of the trough and my head hit the glass of the porthole, nose first, splattering blood everywhere. Somewhat dazed, I stayed where I was, watching horrified as the huge grey mass of water engulfed the entire stern of the ship. The impact propelled me forward, smashing me against the glass again. I staggered away from the porthole, looking at the blood all down my shirt and jacket. To my surprise I felt physically fine; I just needed to get washed, change my clothes and stop the bleeding.

I went below to our deck and ducked into the 'carsie', running the cold tap and splashing the water on my face until eventually the bleeding stopped. However, because of the movement of the ship, bloodstained water was everywhere and must have looked far more dramatic than it was, for when Stretch came in for a leak, he exclaimed 'Christ almighty!' and shot out again. Moments later, Rose appeared and quickly took control. She yelled for some towels, which appeared as if by magic within seconds. She put some of the deck and ordered me to lie on my back.

'I'm fine, Rose, really,' I protested.

'Shut up and lie down,' she asked, still softly but with an edge.

'Nobody did it, Rose. I was looking out the porthole and banged against the glass.'

'Don't give me that rubbish. Someone's been trying their luck haven't they?'

'No, honest, Rose. Go and have a look on the starboard aft hatchway up top. I haven't cleaned it up yet.'

'All right, Cabin. You just stay here for a few minutes and don't move. Understand?'

'Yes Rose,' I promised.

She left and I closed my eyes. It was almost worth a smack in the face with a porthole to have Rose taking such care of me, though I was sure she was angry, despite her soft tone.

She soon reappeared, smiling. 'How on earth did you do it? I can't let you out of my sight for two minutes, can I? What are you grinning at?'

'I thought you were angry at me.'

'I should be! What would your mother say?! Now go and get your head down for a bit. You've got to put the afternoon teas up in half an hour, so shift yourself.'

'I have to clean up the topside alleyway.'

'I've already done it. Go on.'

The rescued men were assigned to our quarters mid-ships, so we had two sleeping on the deck in our cabin. They had no mattress but a couple of blankets and a pillow each. It was from these two that much of our information was gleaned. They seemed to think our accommodation quite grand by comparison with theirs, and after a few beers complained openly about conditions down aft. They also expressed considerable disquiet about the skipper's insistence on running before the sea. The ship could not take much more of it, but he was unmoved. The Mate and the Bosun talked of taking over the ship, and we'd have agreed to anything to stop the hammering we were taking. The deckies blamed it on the skipper having his wife on board – 'Women don't belong on ships; brings bad luck, they do,' was a comment often heard. Added to this the two albatrosses that had been with us had seemingly abandoned us, a sign, we were told with conviction, that we were doomed. Seamen, it appeared, were very superstitious. I had not as yet learned to discount it; rather, it sounded like fact expressed with force and feeling.

On the fourteenth day, however, we emerged into clear skies and a cheerful sea, and all the superstition was forgotten. Though the deadlights were kept down and the rescued crew stayed with us, I felt we'd emerged from a very dark tunnel. Having guests on our cabin deck meant that not only did we get a lot of superstition, but also much insight about what was happening in the Deck Department and with the officers. This gave us a better perspective, even if some of the more extreme speculations were rather dramatic.

Apparently the No. 5 hold tarpaulin covers had been repaired, and some tar used to create a better seal on the planks that formed the hatch until we reached port and things could be repaired properly. The after-accommodation was pumped out and belongings and mattresses rescued – the mattresses put on the hatches to dry in the sun.

One of the able seamen who were our guests explained that we hadn't reached the other side of the hurricane but that we were in the middle, in the eye, which could be fifty to a hundred miles wide.

'Does that mean we've got to go through all that again?' Galley asked in a tone that suggested he might seriously injure the messenger with the wrong answer.

'Probably, but if the captain would turn the ship around and face into the sea, we could be through in much less time,' replied the seaman. 'At least, that's what the chief officer was overheard saying to Sparky on the bridge last night.'

'But how much more can the ship take?' I asked, expecting a precise answer.

'If we keep running before the sea, not much, according to the Bosun. He says we've lost over thirty rivets that he can see, and we're taking on water through the gaps.'

'But there must be thousands of rivets in a ship this size,' I argued. 'And the skipper must know what he's doing.'

'Yes, but if you lose only three or four out of each plate, that whole area gets weakened,' confirmed the other seaman. 'And did you know one of the lifeboats was smashed to pieces and another has been washed away?'

I didn't want to hear anymore. 'I've got to go and serve dinner. C'mon Galley.' So saying, we left them and went down to the galley. Much to our surprise, both Cook and Stretch were already well on the way to getting dinner ready.

'Wow, that looks good,' I said enthusiastically.

'Well, it's time the lads had a decent meal, so let's take advantage of the calm, since it seems it's not going to last,' said Cook. I decided that asking questions had already brought me answers I didn't want to hear, so I would stop asking for now.

Stretch, also in high spirits, added, 'The old man thinks he's like the skippers on the old sailing ships.'

'The deckies reckon there was almost a mutiny, Stretch. Do you believe them?' asked Cook. This conversation was going the wrong way. I grabbed the food tins and headed up to the saloon.

We were not aware of it then, but the first mate, Sparks, and the Bosun had made an official delegation to the captain requesting that he turn the ship and head into the weather until we were clear, because the damage was serious and not much more could be sustained, putting lives on board at unnecessary risk. The captain angrily refused and the deputation insisted that their request was duly noted in the log, which he couldn't refuse. With nothing more to be done, they left the bridge and went about their duties.

The meal was terrific. Cook had really put on a great feast and all on board felt renewed. The cook was the hero of the day, his previous fall from grace forgotten, and all were keen to get into some turps and let out some of the tension of the last two weeks. Even the skipper and his wife came down to the saloon for dinner – only the third time they had done so since leaving Hull.

The following morning we were still only doing about three knots as repairs continued. Though the sky was overcast, the sea was still only slight. Most of the damage to the radio shack had been repaired and some of the equipment was working again. The mattresses were out on deck again, but it would take a strong sun to dry them out. The after accommodation, clear of water now, was still very low due to the increased weight in No. 5 hold, so it was decided that the deck crew would remain   amidships with us until we reached New Zealand. The effect of a good night's sleep and plenty of food worked wonders on all of us, and though we still had some 'rough' to face, we knew we could do it – so long as we didn't need a lifeboat.

At lunch time I looked out of the galley ports aft – the only ones open – and saw the foam-streaked waves building up behind us again. The daylight seemed to have been turned down and there was a cold bite in the air. Much to my delight, one of the albatrosses had returned. He glided mere inches above the surface of the wave, not moving a wing. Suddenly the stillness was broken and the wind came like an invisible hand pushing the tops off the waves into a horizontal, biting rain. The big bird wheeled round and faced into the wind coming from the port stern quarter. He rose up as if on a lift and disappeared from view. 'Here we go again,' I said, turning to face the cook.

'Don't worry, we'll be all right. We're too bad to die,' said Cook.

'You speak for yourself,' I said indignantly, surprised at my own courage. I ducked out of the galley and hurried up to the saloon, where Rose was laying up.

'You'd better put the fiddles up again, Rose; it's coming up behind us fast,' I said quietly, feeling as though a hopeless weight had returned.

'Oh, thank you!' she barked, now having to rearrange settings. 'You're our little weatherman now, are you?'

'No, but honest, you can see it from the galley. It's not far behind.'

'Well go to the galley and see what you can get up here quickly – and take the Second with you!'

I stepped back into the pantry. The Second was getting on the outside of his midday tipple. 'Rose says you are to help me get the food up,' I said rather timidly.

'Oh, does she?' the Second snarled. 'Come on then, move yourself. Let's get it up,' and taking my shoulders he steered me back down to the galley.

'Her ladyship wants the grub up before the weather catches us,' he said to Cook.

'It's all ready; there you are,' said Cook stiffly.

The deck was already pitching steeply, so hurrying was done with caution. One minute we were rushing downhill, the next up a steep incline, all the time rolling from side to side. However, lunch was completed without breakages and we turned in gratefully. Dinner that evening was almost silent.

The following morning saw us back on the mountainous ocean pinnacles, shaking like a cat preparing to attack, our propeller screaming as it left the water. It seemed to last half an hour, but in reality it was probably only a minute or two before we'd slide down again to the foot of the next wave. The difference this time was that the sea was going faster than we were, so after burying our bow in the first wave, the wave astern was catching up with us and overrunning the stern, dumping tons of grey sea on the already battered poop deck and after holds. The sea was like some giant monster and we were a tasty morsel to be devoured, but without hurry – a little play first would sweeten the flavour.

The day wore on into another black and fearsome night, the whole ship shuddering every time the ocean dumped a load on us, the few on board with religious affiliations praying for deliverance. I hoped our deliverance would be on a material plane. I didn't mind going to heaven, but not today, nor even tomorrow. It was strange, really – I found the idea of God as a compassionate and loving father-figure hard to believe in, yet I very much hoped he was there watching over us. Trouble was, his track record was no better than my dad's. And, come to think of it, I had not seen either!

Galley, in a show of bravado, or at least to cheer me up, said, 'Have you heard the latest? The captain is taking us to Hawaii. It's closer than New Zealand. He says we all need a break.'

'No,' I said doubtfully.

'Oh yes,' he confirmed. 'If Honolulu was good enough for the Yanks to choose for sinking ships, it's good enough for me.'

'That's not very funny,' I said. 'We're nowhere near Hawaii. Fiji would be more like it. Though to be honest, I don't really know where we are. I've not been allowed on the bridge for over a week, so I've not been able to have a squizzy at the chart.'

'Ah c'mon, we'll get through it, just like last time,' he answered me.

'And who told you that? Have you got an angel you talk to?' I said, annoyed. 'Anyway, it was the Japs who sunk the American warships.'

'Yes, I know it was. But the president and his staff knew it was going to happen. That's why they moved their carrier fleet out. It was how they got America to join in the war,' said Galley with authority. 'And anyway, you've got to look on the bright side, mate. Those deckies will be in soon – don't want them to think we're scared, do we.'

'Everyone on board's scared; some just don't show it.'

Just then the two deckies came in, followed by Rose.

'We've just lost another lifeboat,' Jerry said. His pal nodded in agreement.

'How do you know?' I asked. 'You're not allowed on deck.'

The Bosun was telling the first and second mates and you can see from up on the bridge. It's almost totally destroyed, so there's only one left now.'

'Who's on the wheel now?' Rose asked. 'I thought the Bosun wouldn't trust anyone else in this.'

'He's got big Jamie on with the second officer standing by, but the Bosun is calling a meeting at ten tomorrow morning in the saloon.'

'What for?' I asked.

Surprisingly, Rose answered. 'Well, the Mate and the Bosun are wanting to turn us round into the sea, and the meeting is to tell us what to do when that happens.'

Galley looked surprised and excited. 'I thought you couldn't turn a ship in a sea this big.'

'Well, said Rose, 'normally they couldn't, but as you know, water's got into the cement and it's increased its weight as concrete and it's like a pendulum. The gamble is that we'll probably go past a 45 degree list as we go round, and we'll get a lot of sea dumped on us while we're over, but as we come around she'll right herself and nose up into the sea, and the ship is designed to take water on the bow, not over the stern.'

Galley closed his mouth, then: 'What's our chance of coming round?'

'I've no idea – I'm not an expert, but it doesn't take an expert to know we're not going to last for long if we keep doing this. Now I suggest you try to get some sleep.' - And pigs should fly.

The lights went out, but I don't think anyone was able to sleep. The sound of the rivets pinging and, ship shuddering under the weight of the crashing sea had us all clinging, white-knuckled to our bunks. Would we survive the turn? We all knew there really was no choice. We would just have to trust the Bridge: they must know what they're doing.

At ten o'clock the following morning all those not on watch squeezed into the saloon.

The first officer, Mr McCloughlin, addressed us. 'At ten-fifteen this morning we are going to "go about". In the conviction that we are currently moving in the same direction as the hurricane, and therefore could still be in it for a long time, and that this ship cannot sustain this punishment much longer, we intend to turn the ship at full speed and round up into the sea. It will be rough for a short while, but we should suffer minimal damage, and I believe we will be out of this within three days. I have to tell you we have lost all radio contact as the shack has now been totally demolished, and three of our four lifeboats are damaged or lost. The sea water contamination in No. 5 has spread to No. 4 and No. 1. I would appreciate a show of hands of those who support this action.'

The cook had heard enough. 'Seems to me, we've no choice. We all know the ship's breaking up.'

'Yeh,' was the cry from several impatient for action.

'Does anyone raise an objection?' asked the mate. There was silence. 'All right,' he went on. 'Your unanimous decision will go into the log. As this is an action contrary to the Skipper's orders. I can't deny. This is not going to be a picnic – all duties will be suspended until we get her around. I suggest you go to your bunks for safety. The ship will heel right over to the starboard and a lot of sea will come on us while we're in that vulnerable position, but we believe she will right herself again, and after that we will be able to keep our nose into the weather. Put your life jackets on and just hang on – do not panic – do not open any water-tight doors. Good luck. Dismissed.'

We made it to our cabin, where complete with lifejackets, we climbed into our pits.

The engines came to full and within five minutes we started the turn, and over she went. There had been almost no talk between us since the meeting. I guess we were all frightened of the task ahead. Now Galley let out a 'Shit! I'm standing on the bloody bulkhead!'

'So this is what it means to be up the wall,' I joked, trying to sound calm and brave, but in reality feeling a strong urge for the toilet. I soon said so.

'You just stay right there and hang on,' said Rose. 'Just think, now you know how a fly feels.'

Just then the ship shuddered terribly under a huge amount of sea crashing down on the exposed port side. We lurched over even further.

'Oh shit, we're going down!' cried Galley.

'Now you shut up,' barked Rose, 'and tell me how long we've been over.'

'I don't know, too bloody long. It's five to eleven,' moaned one of the deckies.

'Why Rose – you got a date?' barked Galley.

'Well, I don't give much for your chances tonight,' I put in.

'Breathe deeply and relax,' said Rose. 'It'll be over a minute.'

'I don't believe you! We're on our way to the bottom and you're saying "breathe deeply chaps!" What a load of crap! We're not going to come up again. I'm leaning on the bloody deckhead, and that means we've gone past forty-five degrees and we're going down. We're bloody sinking.'

The ship shuddered again from yet another wave breaking over us.

'Where are you, Rose?' I pleaded. There was no reply. Then Rose, her mattress and her bedding crashed down to the outer bulkhead. Having no bunk above her, she had little to hang on to. She threw off the pillow and books that had fallen on top of her and struggled to a standing position. The ship gave another huge shudder, and the lights flickered off momentarily. Rose grabbed her pillow for some protection and pushed the mattress off her.

By now we were all completely disoriented: What was up and what was down seemed totally confused. We were standing (or leaning back against the deckhead, mattresses and bedding in disarray around us. We knew that when the ship righted she would go right over the other way, which meant we would fall from the deckhead to the deck and then back up again. How could we avoid getting hurt in the process? Suddenly the starboard bulkhead started to rise and a cheer could be heard from all cabins. However, halfway up she took another pounding and we went over again, though not all the way this time. Slowly – ever so slowly, we started to correct. The ship vibrated as though with supreme effort, and rose and rose till she was upright again. Another cheer went up as she started to lift her bow high to meet the next onslaught – and rolled over in the opposite direction.

A loud cheer again rang through the ship. Except for those on the bridge, no one could actually see the action, only feel it, as the ship was sealed tight, which meant one couldn't anticipate a roll or a pitch in the turn we had just made. The result was that bodies were flung everywhere and perception of up and down quickly became hazy. As we righted, the three of us were sent head over heels into the opposite bulkhead, but eventually things settled down. The cabin was a wreck, mattresses and bedding all adrift. Rose was the only one hurt and was bleeding quite a bit from her arm and temple. I welcome the chance to attend to her wounds for a change – under her detailed instructions, naturally. I was quite surprised to find how firm her muscles were; she wasn't muscular, but fit and wiry.

'You're getting your own back for the Dettol treatment,' she sighed. Rose carried her own medical supplies and was soon bathed and dressed and fully efficient again.

'What time is it, Galley?' she asked.

'Eleven forty-five,' he replied. 'How long were we over do you think?'

'Felt like an age – but probably less than half an hour.'

'Aw c'mon. Ten-fifteen to eleven forty-five – that's an hour and a half,' argued Galley.

'Yes, you're right, you can tell the time, but that was from start to finish. I think you'll find it was not much more than half an hour over the actual turn. The rest was bouncing back to a proper course.'

By midday we were back on duty, our cabin squared away. With no small sense of relief we chattered about the events of the morning. There were several estimates of how long it took us to go about; most agreed it was less than twenty minutes. It was fear that made it seem so much longer.

Despite the success of the operation to turn the ship into the storm, the captain was still not happy, and took the earliest opportunity to recount his displeasure to the first officer.

'That move could have cost the ship and all aboard.'

'Yes, sir, but it didn't. The concrete acted like a pendulum and brought us back up, as I predicted in my written recommendations to you, sir.'

'That's all very well...'

'Anyway, sir, we're not out of the woods yet. The hurricane has carried us a long way north off our course, and without sun, stars or radio we don't know exactly where we are.'

'I thought you took our position while we were in the eye,' snapped the captain, eager to find fault with his first officer.

'Yes sir, we tried, but there was still a lot of cloud both during the day and night, and we could only approximate.'

'Well, where did you think we might be – approximately?' he asked sarcastically. 'I take it you do have some idea. This is very dangerous piece of ocean to get lost in – it's riddled with uncharted atolls and reefs, literally thousands of them, and you stand there telling me you're lost.'

'With all due respect, sir, we were lost, as you put it before we changed course. The last land we saw was Pitcairn Island. If I'm correct, I believe we're now within fifty miles off Eastern Samoa.'

'We can't be that far off course. I suggest you try a little harder with your maths, Number One.'

'It doesn't alter the fact that we're sailing almost blind. However, if we maintain this south south-west course I believe we'll break free of this weather and be in clear sea in the shortest possible time.'

'Tell me Number One, what do you calculate, or should I say guess, as shortest possible time?'

'Forty-eight hours, sir,' and with that he turned on his heel and left the skipper fuming.

As it happened, within thirty-six hours the winds were down to gale category and visibility was three to five miles from the bridge – a huge improvement from barely being able to see past the bow. Life on board was quickly returning to normal. The only different was the Mate was now everyone's hero and no one trusted the skipper anymore. We were all in a celebratory mood.

Deadlights were still down, and nine of us were squeezed into the cook's cabin. 'C'mon Cabin, get it down you. It's only gin, so you won't get a headache, if that's what you're frightened of. You've drowned it in lemonade anyway,' said Cook.

'It's all right for you; your drink it like water,' I replied, thinking of the cook's ability to consume two bottles a day.

'His mother used to put a teat on the gin bottle,' jibed Stretch. 'You can tell by the way he sucks it down – and he's teaching Galley to drink like a fish.'

'Ah, piss off,' said Galley jovially. 'You can't talk, you put away at least a bottle a day. You'll finish up with a big red hooter like the alkies down the Mile End road.'

With everyone smoking and drinking like there was no tomorrow, the jokes got more bawdy and everyone seemed to be talking at once. I wondered who was listening and, with the excuse of a leak, I unsteadily climbed over legs and backs to get out.

The alley smelt of good clean diesel – a country road with flowers couldn't be sweeter. I still couldn't get on deck, so I went to our cabin. The two seamen were asleep already, as was Rose by the look of it.

'You'll do well out of there,' Rose voice said from behind her curtain. 'They'll be at it still the small hours and I suppose Galley's tucking it away.'

'Yes, but he's having fun, and he just doesn't seem to get drunk.'

'It's no good for that arm of his; he could lose it in Dunedin,' said Rose. 'But you can't talk to him. He thinks he's a big man because he can drink so much. I suppose some people's blood must be different.' I jumped up into my bunk and lay back. My head started to spin and I welcome the dark abyss of sleep.

The following morning before doing the dhobiing I climbed the two flights to the bridge. This was the only way I could find out what the outside world looked like, and taking a coffee up to the officer or watch gained me brief access to the bridge and a news update. The second officer was on the port wing looking out through his glasses at some islands we had just passed. It was still dark at 5.10am, but behind the islands the sky was already light green where the sun would come up before six.

I walked quietly to the chart table and followed the pencil line marking our position. There seemed to be so many islands with unpronounceable names.

'I've brought you some coffee, sir,' I said, making my way to the wing before he caught me snooping.

'Oh, thank you, Cabin. That's very thoughtful of you.' His Glasgow dialect sounded quite comforting. I wasn't sure why, but perhaps it allowed me to forget that we were a long way from home.

'What are the islands, sir?'

'Uta Vava'u, if I'm correct, in which case we should pass Tofua to starboard before midday.'

"When do think we will reach New Zealand"

'Oh at a guess I'd say in about ten days, but we may not go straight to Dunedin. We might go to Auckland to get this concrete taken out and some repairs done. We have to get the lifeboats and radio repaired at the first port that can do it, and I'd say that's Auckland.

He finished the coffee and handed me the mug back. 'Thank you, sir,' I said, trying to hide my excitement.

'If you want to keep informed, young Cabin, bring a coffee for the helmsman as well in future. Do you think you could do that?'

'Yes, of course, sir,' I said, looking at the helmsman.

In two minutes I was back with a mug of coffee which I placed on the cabinet behind the helmsman, an A.B. Seaman with bright ginger hair called Carrots. No one, it seemed, even in the Deck Department, was called by their given names, and if their job or physical features didn't suggest a name, it was usually where they were from – Brum or Leedsy, Scouse or Jock. Only officers were called Michael or William! Carrots were grateful for the coffee. He still had almost an hour to stand at the helm and keep awake. The four to six watch was the least popular.

I ducked down below again and called by the cabin to tell Galley the news, but his bunk hadn't been slept in and the others were still 'fast on'. Quietly I pulled the door to and went to get on with the cook's dhobiing and my scrub-out.

Later that morning the deadlights were raised and ports opened. It was as though we had come through from the underworld; now we were free and a fresh breeze blew through the ship. Spirits quickly soared, even for those with thick heads.

Astern, the grey-black sky was a reminder of the last twenty-one days in the path of the hurricane and how far off course to the north we'd gone with it. Ahead, the sparkling diamonds were back on the deep blue sea. From this point we could see both extremes, and were very glad to be passing into finer weather; even the two albatrosses had returned. I wondered if they'd ever really left – maybe they came on board somewhere and got their heads down till we were out of it. They certainly looked no worse for wear. I went down to the stern with some bread, but they were not overly impressed, snatching the bread I threw without any apparent effort.

They flew up close to where I was standing, the draught from the ship's movement allowing them to hang in the air just out of arm's reach, huge wings outstretched, their eyes missing nothing, including me. The nearest one appeared to be looking straight at me.

I wondered what they were thinking – perhaps they wondered what I was thinking. I wondered if they liked me – I certainly liked them. It occurred to me that they had looked after us, and they seemed to exude wisdom. Perhaps I was allowing my imagination to run away a bit, but I found the words hard to formulate in my mind. I felt they were totally aware of themselves and their environment; maybe they didn't have thoughts – they just knew. If only I could stop trying to think and just be aware, like them. I gave in – or at least that's what it felt like – and I felt a tingling rush of Joy that rang through every cell of my being. I was so happy a tear ran down my cheek. It was as though time stood still. For a few precious moments I had shared the clarity the birds had. I don't know how long I stood there; it was so wonderful I wanted it never to end, but that thought brought me back to myself. Half an hour? Perhaps only a few minutes. The birds lifted in unison high above the stern, turned to wheel down and swept across another wave. I walked quietly back amidships. Could I tell anyone? – Nah, they'd think I'd flipped. For now I thought I'd better just keep it to myself.

Nine days later, dawn revealed New Zealand's Great Barrier Island rising out of a shimmering sea on our port bow, its bush-covered mountains disappearing into low white clouds. It was most impressive. I would not have been surprised if long canoes full of warriors had paddled out to greet us.

'Come here, Cabin, take a butcher's at this one,' called Galley from the starboard side. I clambered over the hold and saw Little Barrier, a smaller island whose sheer cliffs rose straight up into the clouds.

Perhaps it was because we hadn't seen land for so long, but this was truly magical and answered all my dreams of exciting foreign lands. The next hour had me excitedly bobbing in and out to the deck to glimpse the many islands as we arrive in Auckland. The second mate had told me of the volcano Rangitoto which stood guard over the harbour, and it was all he had promised and more. I could see Captain Cook going ashore here – in fact, I could see Henry Morgan, Robinson Crusoe and Man Friday in my imagination.

This was the stuff – this was worth the hardships.

The sea was like glass, though we were still rolling with the pendulum effect of the concrete while we awaited the pilot. Eventually, the rolling subsided and we proceeded up the channel to round North Head a little before 9am. By 9.45 we were alongside on Bledisloe Wharf with shore officials crawling all over the ship, looking at the mess and writing things on clipboards.

* * *

CHAPTER 13

Time to go to Sydney

Two days later the drilling started. Shore workers with pneumatic drills were breaking up the concrete in Nos. 5, 4 and 1 and a cloud of dust covered everything. Chippies came on and rebuilt the radio shack and new equipment was installed. The remains of the old one, already encrusted in green dried salt, was torn out.

Galley was whipped into the Auckland Hospital to have his infected arm treated as soon as we docked. They lanced his arm and drew off all the fluid, talking of gangrene and all sorts of things, but he was out in less than a week with lots of pills, having been told to stay off the booze and away from women, neither of which he had any intention of doing. He reckoned he was so full of antibiotics he couldn't get another dose. I was very glad to have his cheerful chatter back again.

When Galley came back from hospital, we went ashore together. For me it was the first dry land since England – it felt really great. Most of the buildings were fewer than four storeys high. The effect was much less threatening than London, where houses were that high and commercial buildings often ten storeys. The most noticeable feature on the main streets was that the entire pavement was covered by a sort of roof that hung from the front of the shops, presumably to allow shoppers to stay dry when it rained. The buildings themselves seemed to house mainly clothes shops, banks and insurance companies. There seemed to be no furniture shops, restaurants, car show rooms or grocery shops. Two or three shop sold what they call 'Manchester', which, it transpired, was linen. We later discovered a shop with the strange name 'The Farmers', which sold everything, rather like 'Gamages' in London, and because it was three blocks off the main drag, they provided a free bus ride to it. This seemed a pretty good idea, and gave us a mini tour around a few city blocks.

The people were friendly, the milkshakes super. We went to see 'The Robe' at the Civic, a cinema that was in experience in itself. A large organ rose out of the floor and played popular tunes, a pair of lions blinked their red eyes and we were surrounded with make-believe temples, their turrets reaching up into a star-studded sky. We had never seen a cinema like this; it almost made the film irrelevant as it caught our young imaginations and took us on journeys of fantasy.

When the film started I felt interrupted, but soon the action was enough to keep us engrossed for over two hours. Though we were both impressed, Galley was yearning for some action of a more personal nature. So after another great milkshake we strolled down Queen Street discussing girls. It was not long before we were accosted by two very attractive young ladies, who invited us to their party. They took our hands and, crossing the road, led us through a doorway and up some stairs. They were laughing, smiling and encouraging. Galley thought he'd arrived in heaven, especially as no one had mentioned a price.

At the top of the stairs was another doorway and we found ourselves in a large room full of people seated in rows and rows of chairs. The two men inside the door took our arms and steered us, smiling but firmly, to some vacant seats among a lot of other men. The girls had been directed to the other side, which was all women – which was not quite what we had in mind.

'Let us pray!' The man in a black suit said at the front.

'We've been conned,' said Galley in a stage whisper. 'It's a bloody church service.' He was right, but there was no escape. The big door we'd come through was closed and one of the ushers was standing beside it with his hands together in front of him. Obviously he was there to make sure non-believers didn't escape. It went on and on; we stood and sang, we sat while the man at the front went on about 'the gnashing of teeth and everlasting purgatory'. He seemed so full of anger. His face was all puffed up and red and he had enormous teeth. I thought he could well bite you if you disagreed. We sang some more and prayed some more. Galley kept telling me what he thought of some of the strange people who were there. And we were both giggling like a pair of schoolgirls, much to the annoyance of the very serious audience, and one lady in particular, who Galley insisted looked a dead ringer for Churchill with a moustache!

At last they let us go. We burst out of there with Olympian vigour, down the stairs and out into the freedom of the street, gulping in the profane fresh air.

'If you ever open your mouth on this little adventure, I'll make you wish you hadn't,' Galley said, clutching my shirt.

'Oh, you needn't worry,' I said. 'It would earn us both a lot of scorn.' So we finished up at the Mission to Seamen as usual, and had a game of snooker before returning to the ship sober and unsullied.

Upon our arrival, a telephone had been connected on board in the saloon and, much to my surprise, it rang as I was laying up after breakfast. As I was the only one in the saloon I answered and a female voice asked for William Smith. 'I'm sorry,' I said, 'I don't know a William Smith.' I was thinking about how, in reality, I knew very few people's real names, when the Second burst in and demanded: who is it?

'A lady asking for William Smith.'

'That's okay, it's for me. Go and get yourself a mug of tea,' he said dismissively. I left and thought no more about it.

Now, a few days later back on board, things started slowly to make more sense as a young woman, obviously quite drunk, giggled her way out of the Second's cabin with him in tow. 'C'mon, you two pricks,' slurred the Second, 'these girls are going to give us a show.'

Full of curiosity, we followed them around to the small crew mess on the port side, which we seldom used. It was already full and three other girls were embracing some of the crew, including Cook, who seemed to be devouring his partner, a woman obviously somewhat older than the rest. We all squeezed in and someone passed us a bottle of beer each. 'There's plenty of gin if you'd rather,' said one of the deckies who'd bunked down with us in the storm.

'Nah, she's right,' said Galley, obviously trying to sound like a native.

'What would you boys like?' said the girl who had come out of the Second's cabin.

'Swallow the bottle,' someone yelled, and others urged 'Yeh!

Yeh!'

The girl was enthusiastically helped up on to the table and a full bottle of Coke was thumped onto the table with its cap off. The radio blared music, as girl danced, or rather writhed, on the table to animated support from the audience. Lifting her skirt high, she came lower and lower, absorbing almost the whole bottle. The lads cheered and she reached to grasp hold of the bottom of the bottle, continuing to sway and writhe till she was free of it.

'Okay, big boys, who wants it?' Several lunged at once and hungrily devoured the contents between them, the Cook being the greediest. He offered me a swig and I reeled back in horror, much to the amusement of everyone. Galley, on the other hand, was keen to show he was a man and begged for a swig, but he was too late. The Coke bottle was empty!

'Never mind, dear. I'll give you a special later,' she said, kissing Galley very fully on the mouth as he eagerly responded. The memory of VD films at the Vindi helped me extricate myself from the room. I'm sure no one noticed my departure and I headed towards the hatch and some fresh air on deck. I had not yet crossed the bridge to manhood. However as I passed the Pantry, the aroma drew me in.

I was happy to find Rose making a toasted sandwich. 'Have you been in the mess?' she enquired rather crossly.

'Yes, but I didn't Join in anything.'

'Good for you. I suppose Galley's down there, boots an' all?'

'Yes, and enjoying himself,' I said defensively.

'I think you mean he can't wait to get another dose. How many girls are there, Cabin?'

'Four. The Cook's got one to himself, and so has the Second, and there's two younger ones.'

'Well, you just stay clear, d'yer understand? They'll probably stay on board around the coast and get off in Dunedin.'

'Do the officers know this goes on?' I asked in astonishment.

'Yes, of course, though I imagine the skipper's wife will take a dim view if she sees them.'

'What are you making, Rose? It smells smashing.'

'Do you want me to make you one?'

'Yeah, that would be great,' I replied, suddenly becoming aware that I hadn't eaten.

'Okay, well, you hard boil these four eggs and give me the yolks when they're done.' Rose cut two doorstep slices of bread, toasted them, then spread the solid yolks on with lashings of butter and salt, topped with grated cheese, which she place under the grill. I made some coffee and we tucked into our little midnight feast. I felt safe with Rose, and she never came on to me. So, for now I could put off any decision about becoming a man.

It took more than two weeks to get the concrete out and at last our ship once again sat upright and level in the water. Two lifeboats had been supplied and we were due to collect the third in Port Chalmers.

The girls remained on board as Rose had said. Their lives seemed quite a contrast to the life ashore where, it seemed, most people were rather religious. There were churches on every corner – like pubs in England. Doorways between shops had signs which said Bible Study Classes or named some strange-sounding church or missionary society. Of course, there were pubs, though these were usually hotels and they seemed to take their drinking as seriously as their religion. They were not the cosy, picturesque or character pubs of England. In contrast, most people stood up to drink, sometimes at small high tables where they rested their jars of beer. The talk was mainly about racing, rugby, unionism or work. The beer was cold and went down very easily in the warm weather, though it was clear that many had no trouble getting it down, no matter the day, because at 6pm the pubs shut! So many customers obviously wanted to consume as much as they would have if the pub had stayed open till 10 o'clock. For those who worked till 5 o'clock, this gave them only one hour in which to achieve this, which meant buying a huge full jug and a glass...each!

By 6.15pm the city centre was almost deserted. Everything closed and there was little to do. At the weekend everything except the cinema was closed, which prompted the saying, 'Would the last one leaving New Zealand please switch out the light.' For all that, Auckland seemed a paradise to live in, and I vowed one day, when I'd had enough travel, to come here to live.

During our two weeks in Auckland, we walked up and down

Queen Street quite a few times and enjoy some fabulous milk shakes, but never met any girls – that is to say ordinary, nice girls. Galley went to the Bridgeway Tavern and a place downstairs in a big hotel at the bottom of Queen Street to satisfy his needs. He would regale us with the details, but though his descriptions sounded really great, the images of the VD films still haunted me.

It was soon time to put to sea again and head down to Dunedin and the South Island where, five days later, we berthed at Port Chalmers to unload most of our cement. We then moved up to Dunedin to revittle the ship. We were tied up just ahead of a smaller ship called the 'Gothic', on which the newly crowned Queen Elizabeth and her husband were touring, but we didn't see her and she didn't come to see us.

Dunedin was different from subtropical Auckland, with its stone building and shops selling tartan cloth. We might well have been in Aberdeen: we even saw a couple of guys in tartan kilts! Whether that was because the queen was in town, I don't know. But the atmosphere was much more provincial and the locals even more friendly.

We plucked up courage on Saturday night and went to the dance at the Town Hall. It was just like at home, boys on one side, girls down the other, and the band was playing tunes they had obviously played for years. I made several attempts at asking girls to dance, but after they had witnessed my abilities on the floor, they turned away and giggled or said they were sitting this one out. In fact, most of the girls did dance rather well, and it was clear I had some learning to do. The feeling of inadequacy and rejection wasn't helped when Galley disappeared early with a tall, willowy girl. I finished up strolling back to the ship alone. It was so quiet. No cars, no buses and no people, just me, it seemed, strolling along the wharf. They must all go to bed very early.

Much to my surprise no one caught a dose off the girls who had been on board around the coast. Their presence was not something that could be kept secret. One day the Cook ordered his afternoon tea and when I took it in, he offered me his bed, complete with woman.

'Come on, Cabin, it's time you lost your virginity. Carmen here will show you what you're missing. Won't you, love?'

'Yes, come on. You're the cabin boy, aren't you? Don't be shy.

Climb in here and let me show you a good time!'

'Thank you, but I can't today. I've got to wash Cook's whites,' I said.

'Sod the whites, they can wait,' said Cook. 'Carmen's kindly offered to assist in your education.'

'Er, no thanks, honest. You're very nice, but no, I've got to go.' I was out of there. The cabin door didn't seem keen to open, but eventually I was out, their laughter ringing in my ears and the strong odours of the room clinging to me. I rushed out on deck and grabbed the rail. That was a very narrow escape, and I was trembling, and I couldn't seem to stop it. I took some deep breaths, squeezed my eyes shut and thought of scrubbing the floor. Eventually the shaking subsided and I went back inside to my duties. The memory haunted me for several years, though with the passing of time it did occasionally change from fear to fantasy.

The following day we slipped out of Dunedin, rounded Foveaux Strait by early evening and set our bow for Australia. Long, rolling swells came up from the south and carried us with good speed, albeit in an apparently drunken fashion.

The rumours spread through the ship as to where we were headed, some said we could pick up a cargo in Australia and go home via the Suez Canal; other said we were going to work the Aussie coast, running iron ore. My favourite was that we were to Honolulu to take on pineapples! On Friday at 10am the crew were assembled on No. 4 hold and addressed by the skipper.

'Men – we've seen some tough times together. Well, good news: we're about to have it easy. This ship has been leased to the Australian government for a period of twenty months, to run iron ore between Port Kembla, Whyalla and Thursday Island. You will receive an extra seven shillings a week 'ore' bonus, a nice easy run and plenty of opportunity for bronzing. That's all – dismissed.' For those of us who were not familiar with iron ore and the ports mentioned, the air was full of questions. It sounded quite a promising tour, though a long one.

Back in the cabin, which we now had to ourselves again, both Galley and I leapt upon Rose. 'Tell us Rose, what are those ports like?'

'Get off! You're like a pair of randy dogs after a bitch on heat.'

'Well, we know you're always on heat,' retorted Galley.

'That's enough from you, you big stick man, you. You'll know soon enough what iron ore's like: it's red or black and gets into everything. Your clothes, your food – that's why you get the shilling a day.'

'That's not bad, though, is it? My eight pounds a month will be nine pounds fifty.'

'Well, you've got no choice now,' said Galley. 'They're not going to ring you up and ask "What cargo Rose would like this time".

'You know, a shilling a day isn't worth it. Ten shilling a day wouldn't be worth it. That's why so many crew jump ship. And those ports! All twelve-hour quickies – in, out and wipe it jobs. You two can forget about shore leave – and anyway, they're hellholes. There's nothing at any of them. I can't go on, I really can't.' I'd never seen Rose like this: it was quite a shock. She was by far the bravest among us, yet here she was, almost in tears. It had an unsettling effect on me, and caused me to question how things were going to be.

'Oh, you'll be fine, Rose. Just think of all those big Australians,' Galley jibed before ducking quickly out of the cabin. One of the Rose's shoes hit the door with a thud.

'You wouldn't jump ship, would you Rose?' I asked, somewhat concerned.

'Listen, Cabin, if anyone were going to jump ship, they would have keep it strictly to themselves. Even good friends will dob you in to protect their own skin. Now, subject closed. I don't want to hear another word about it. Do you understand?'

'Yes, Rose.' But I was not happy. If Rose left, the Second would remove the rest of my teeth for starters. Yet she'd made it clear she didn't want to talk about it. What if I wanted to go? How would I go about it? Who could I ask? Who could I trust? If Rose was right, there was no one. The prospect was scary, yet exciting. I wondered if Rose might take me, for it seemed clear she was going, but she'd shut me out. I felt rejected and unable to express it. I had better sort myself out, and smartly. In forty-eight hours we would reach Sydney. I needed money, clothes and how to get ashore. Strolling down the gangway with a suitcase may not get me far. I figured out how I could do it. At tomorrow's sub, I could draw £5, and that was probably all I had. Although my wage was £8 a month, 15/- a week went to my mother and then there was tax and national health stamps, so I figured £5 would be the limit. Although it had been almost sixteen weeks since we left Hull, our long stay in Auckland had badly dented my ship's account.

I could wear two pairs of trousers, three shirts, a jacket and raincoat; that way I wouldn't have to carry a bag, and though I didn't smoke I could buy a carton of 555s to trade if required: that wouldn't be noticed.

After the end of the war, in 1949 or 1950, some people who lived two doors away from us in England had emigrated on a £10 deal to Brisbane. Michael, the son, would be pleased to see me, I felt sure, and Brisbane was just up a bit on the coast north of Sydney. I'd catch the train and call in on him, see if he could offer me a job. It dawned on me that, without realising it, I had made the decision to jump ship. The thought of should or shouldn't I hadn't really come into it. There really wasn't a choice.

When I awoke on Monday morning we were alongside already, on a bunkering jetty. Not far away to the right, the Sydney Harbour Bridge towered above us, leading over to the city of Sydney. I had butterflies in my stomach, but I had to ensure no one knew what I was up to. I just did everything as normal.

I waited until after lunch when everyone had either gone ashore or was asleep and without a word to anyone, my heart banging away loud enough to hear, I went to the gangway. There was no one there, so I slipped quickly ashore and turned right, heading for Sydney – and freedom.

* * *

CHAPTER 14

Sydney

The harbour bridge ahead led straight to the city centre, where I was sure I could catch a train to Brisbane. The temperature was much hotter than I had expected – in the nineties – and my two vests and pants, three shirts, jacket and a rain coat soon proved to be a burden. Matters were made considerably worse when I realised that though I thought I was walking towards Sydney and the bridge, I was actually on a finger of land that went nowhere – a bunkering quay ending in a very small park jutting out into Sydney harbour.

One thing was obvious, I couldn't risk trying to walk back again past the ship – I would be spotted straight away. The only option was to hide in the park until nightfall, then make for the nearest rail station. I found a group of bushes and climbed into the middle. This gave me much needed shade and seclusion.

Much of my fear of being caught was probably unnecessary, since I had spoken to no one of my intention to jump ship. No one would worry until just before sailing – or at least till dinner time. I wondered if anyone else had jumped. Certainly I had heard no mention of it from anyone. It was not a subject I'd ever heard discussed, except that one brief time from Rose. All I knew was that if she had gone I could not bear to take any more beatings from the Second. I didn't know what Australia was going to be like, but I knew it had to be better than two years on board the Princess Tara with daily abuse assured and no shore leave.

It was getting terribly hot – all my clothes were soaked in perspiration and only an hour had passed. It would be at least another three hours before it was dark enough to slip past the ship unseen.

I thought about Michael Cummings in Brisbane and how surprised he would be to see me. He'd probably be eighteen or nineteen by now, and well able to tell me where I could find a Job. I would jump on the first train and be there, if not tonight, then by tomorrow morning, and all I'd need would be a telephone directory. His mother might not be pleased to see me, but his sister Sally would – we all used to play in the same gang, named 'The Moth Club' because we would all meet in secret at Barries Garage Loft by the light of a candle, and without fail would be joined by a sizeable moth or two, attracted by the flame.

At long last the sun went down and the lights came on, casting long black shadows along the wharf: adequate cover for me to work my way behind the buildings and bunkering pipes and past the ship. At the wharf gates a lorry was stopped, having its papers cleared, which made it easy for me to slip past quietly and walk up the hill to Waverley station. Fortunately, it was almost deserted. I went up to the ticket window for my train to Brisbane. The sallow-complexioned man said, 'Twelve pounds, sonny,' with a doubtful expression on his face.

'I've only five pounds,' I replied. 'How far will that get me?'

'Newcastle is two pounds, sixteen shillings,' he grunted impatiently, looking over his glasses.

'Is it on the way to Brisbane?'

'Yes, but you've still a way to go from Newcastle,' he assured me.

'Never mind, it'll have to do. I'll take it.' I pushed my only large white fiver towards him. He took it in both hands and swung around on his stool to hold it up to the light, then back again to bury it in the drawer in front of him. He pressed some well-worn brass buttons and up shot the ticket.

'Change at City Hall.' He counted out my change of £2.40. 'Be along soon. Platform Two.'

'Thank you.' I climbed over to the other platform, hoping there would be no one else from the ship waiting to go into the city. Fortunately there wasn't.

The train soon rattled in. It was quite full and I looked for a corner in which to be less conspicuous, if that were possible. Being so overdressed, with my raincoat black with sweat, I must have looked very odd – people stared, three girls twittered, but no one said a word as we noisily rumbled over the bridge into Sydney proper, the whole journey taking no more than ten minutes. The train squealed to a halt and I was swept off with the crowd, most of whom were going out on the town. I looked for the Newcastle train, which was due to leave at 9.30pm. I had plenty of time to get on the outside of a big banana milkshake which, considering I'd had nothing to eat since lunch, barely touched the sides going down.

The Newcastle train turned out to be the Brisbane express. The thought did occur that it would be good if I didn't have to get off at Newcastle.

At 9.30 we got under way. Sometime between 10 and 11pm we stopped up in the mountains at a remote station beside a lake. Under the platform light I saw two policemen boarding the train. My guilty conscience assumed they were after me: after all, the station master at Waverley would easily identify me. There was no choice – I'd have to get off the train. I made my way to the end of the carriage, the whistle blew and I dropped down to the stones at the side of the track and ran with the train for cover till I was clear of the station. There I dived down the bank, watching the rear light of the train disappear into the night.

I sat just below the track line for a while in the absolute darkness and silence. I felt alone in a way that was quite different from anything I'd experienced before. I didn't feel lonely, but free. The lights from the station had been switched off and the night was lit with twinkling stars. In the moonlight the lake shone like silver and strange animals began to emerge from the stillness. I couldn't see them. But I could hear their movements. I hoped there were no snakes.

Cautiously, I started to make my way down through the tall gum trees towards the lake. The screeches from unseen animals or birds combined with the shadows to give me the willies. It was a relief when, after little more than an hour, I eventually made the shore. As I looked out across the water I felt as if I were the first person to discover this place.

'Yer weren't thinking of swimming it were yer, mitey?' asked a gravelly voice just behind me.

I almost jumped out of my skin. 'Where did you come from?'

'More's the point, where did you come from? Yer sounded like a herd of bleeding elephants coming through the bush, scaring all the natives.'

From what I could see the man looked to be in his fifties with a very weathered face. His long, grey hair was tied with elastic behind his neck. His clothes were loose and shabby, his pants tied with string above his ankles. In the poor light he looked like a beggar. The only thing we had in common was a raincoat. His though, was old and quite torn.

'What natives?' I asked, alarmed at the thought of a tribe of Aborigines peering unseen from the dark.

'No, not abos – the wildlife. It's their house you just blundered through.'

'Is that why they made so much noise?' I enquired, 'What are they?'

'Well, let's see. There's kookaburras, possums, koalas for a start, frogs, galahs and roos. Have you ever seen any of them?'

'No, sir. I only arrived in Australia today.'

'Where are you from, boy? Not a bloody "pom", I hope.'

'I just arrived by ship today from New Zealand,' I replied, not wanting to lie, but giving him an acceptable answer. I remembered a conversation in the saloon about how the Australians didn't think much of the 'poms'.

'I'd just got me head down, and you wake me up with all your noise. You're a city boy, that's for sure. C'mon, I'll put the billy on.'

I followed him to his spot less than forty feet back in the trees. I must have blundered right past him without knowing. He poked about in the ashes of the fire and, adding a few twigs, soon had his billy hanging over a good little flame.

'Where're you headed, kid – do you know?'

'Yes, I'm going to Newcastle, then on to Brisbane to meet a friend.'

'Oh that's good. Does your friend know you're coming?' he asked, after some thought.

'Well no, not yet, but he'll be pleased to see me.'

'What's your name boy?'

'Joe,' I said before I could stop myself. I realised, too late, that I had said too much already.

'Well, Joe, if you ask me, you've jumped off a pommy ship in Sydney and you haven't got a clue how to survive. Now you tell me if I'm wrong.' He poured the strong tea and passed it to me. I didn't know what to say so I hid behind the tin mug of tea.

'What's your name?' I eventually asked.

'Salty, and I'm right, aren't I? It's all right. I'm not going to dob you in. Look, I left a wife and two screaming kids in Adelaide, and I likes being free to go me own way.'

'Why do they call you Salty if you weren't at sea?'

'Well, when I was a young 'un, I got a reputation for telling stories. I used to make them up from different ones I'd heard on the wireless. Later when I was droving, the lads used to get me pissed to tell 'em stories. Well, they just got longer and longer, and they reckoned I must have been an old sailor in a past life! To be straight, I don't know much about such things and I've no time for the bible bashers. One day, though, I'll write a book and put some of me stories in it.'

The smoke from the fire was making my eyes sore and I was feeling very tired. Salty, noticing me rubbing them, gathered up some fronds and leaves. He chuckled.

'Okay, boy, you can kip down here and tomorrow will see what's to do, but for now, rub these eucalyptus leaves on your face and hands, or the mozzies will be after you when the smoke dies away.'

When I awoke the following morning, the sun and Salty were already up. In fact, Salty was nowhere to be seen. I stumbled down to the lake for a wash, peeling off my layers of clothing until I was stripped to the waist. I splashed the surprisingly cold water over me and dried myself with one of my vests.

I sat on a small boulder and looked across the still water. Already the sun was making the far shore shimmer in the heat. It was very quiet. I felt my breathing slow down after the shock of the cold water. I closed my eyes, remaining conscious of the decreasing movement of my abdomen as Rose had taught me, and had got me to do almost every day on board. I had come to find the practice gave me confidence and I was determined to keep it up every day, if possible. I had been sitting for less than half an hour, thoroughly enjoying the difference of doing it ashore surrounded by different smells and sounds, when a different sound startled me back to the more mundane.

'You're a walk-in bloody wardrobe,' said Salty from right behind me.

'How come I never hear you walking up behind me?' I enquired.

'Well if I clopped about like you, I'd never eat, for a start,' retorted Salty. 'Speaking of which, come and have some breakfast. I suppose you'd like egg and bacon?'

Salty rustled about and had the fire going in no time. I gathered some sticks to keep it going and watched, amazed, as he poured some rice into the almost boiling water in the pan, then produced an egg out of each of his raincoat pockets. From an inside pocket came half a wrinkled green pepper, which he sliced and added to the pot, stirring the whole lot until it was like an omelette. He then cut it in two and flipped half on to a tin plate.

'Here you are, boy. It's got to last you all day, so don't waste any.' So saying, he got stuck into his half, which was still in the pan.

After the meal I gave him a packet of cigarettes by way of thanking him. His eyes lit up with open appreciation.

I spent the whole day walking with him through the bush and listening to his stories. He showed me parrots with bright red and green bodies and long tails, and the big white ones he called galahs. We didn't see a kangaroo – he said they preferred the greener places – but possums were everywhere, and the racket they made at night was awful. Salty said they would steal any food if you left it out. He caught a rabbit, which, to my horror, turned out to be our dinner, though by then my squeamishness was overtaken by hunger. As soon as it was dark he disappeared again, and came back with four potatoes and a handful of runner beans.

'Never take more than you need,' he said, putting them on the ground in front of me. 'You can get them peeled and into the pot.' I set to willingly. All round, the tall ghost gums stood like silent soldiers. They were so still, yet I knew there was a lot of wildlife among them that I couldn't see and wasn't keen to ask about.

Salty impressed me. Despite his bedraggled appearance, he had the qualities of a magician. He was no taller than me, and looked almost pitiful in his shabby clothes; yet they hid a well educated man of some unique abilities. One minute he was there with you, then he was gone; no by-your-leave, just gone. His return was the same: he could suddenly reappear and produce food like a magician, a rabbit out of an empty hat. I knew, of course, that he wasn't a magician, just a skilful thief, but he had a rugged gentleness that made him somehow special.

After dinner, instead of telling me his colourful stores of past adventures, real or otherwise, he became serious. 'Tomorrow morning you're getting back on that train to Newcastle. There's no future for you here in the bush, anyway I likes me own company and you've to find your young friend.'

'But I could stay just a few more days with you, couldn't I? It's great being free from authority and I love your stories.'

'Don't argue, you've a train to catch,' he said.

The following morning he put me on the train and I quietly found a seat. I turned to wave good bye, but he'd gone again. He'd said he had little time for farewells, but as the train pulled out I strained to catch a glimpse of him. I felt hot tears well up and I quickly thought of other things.

I'd left him my raincoat and a shirt under a bush, and a note tucked in his little stash telling him where they were. I thanked him for looking after me and wished him the best. I knew we'd never meet again. It seemed strange: I left all those on the boat without a backward glance, yet I'd known Salty for less than two days and I missed him already.

The only item other than clothing and cigarettes that I'd brought off the ship was my diary, and events had made writing in it difficult. However, now I could do some catching up. I wondered if anyone else had jumped ship, and put down Rose, and maybe Carrots. He had some family – cousins, I thought – in Melbourne, so Whyalla might be closer. I couldn't think of anyone else. Galley surely would have said something if he'd been going to. I knew if I were caught I could face six months imprisonment for desertion and illegal entry; sometimes they even made men work in the sugar cane up to their waist in water and leeches. I didn't fancy either of those. I must try not to get caught. I thought, I should write to mum and tell her I'm okay, but then she might worry. Better to wait till I get a job and can send her some money. She probably won't get any more from the ship, and that won't please her. Still, I'll send her some when I get to Brisbane.

* * *

CHAPTER 15

Newcastle

The train conductor was very talkative and not at all suspicious. He had a ruddy complexion, which made him appear a good bit younger than he probably was. His wire-framed glasses, perched on the end of his cherry nose, completed the impression that he would look perfect in a Santa outfit.

'The station before Newcastle Central – will you tell me when we get there?'

'Why's that then? Your mum meeting you?'

'No, I'm going to stay with my friend, and he might meet me.'

'Okay, son, I'll let you know when we're almost there.' He turned and waddled away up the carriage to talk to two girls who seemed to do nothing but giggle. My plan was to avoid any waiting police by getting off at a suburban station and walking into town to find the YMCA.

Eventually Santa waddled back and said, 'We're just coming into your station now.' I looked out the window, seeing nothing but a rather barren landscape and only the occasional homestead.

'Oh. Well, I hope he's here,' I said, trying to sound confident amid much squealing of brakes and hissing steam. I jumped down on to the plat form. To my surprise, no one else got off. I looked around and realised that, whilst in England the train would make several suburban stops before the main station, in Australia, suburban meant a long way out. The town had less than a dozen building and only one shop, a general store. There I could ask directions and treat myself to an ice cream – it was 2.45pm and more than a little warm.

'Just follow this road: it'll take you to the main street of Newcastle,' the lady in the flowery apron said as he handed my ice cream and change. 'But it's a fair step. There's a bus at six.'

'Oh, that's okay. I like walking,' I replied. And I did – at least for the first mile.

It was very hot. The road wasn't sealed and seemed to carry little traffic. There were no houses at all, just dry hills of stones and scrub and the odd eucalyptus tree. As I walked, I thought of my prospects. Clearly, my remaining £2 wasn't going to get me to Brisbane. I would either have to hitch or get a job, and earn at least £10 for the fare to Brisbane. I wondered how long that might take. On the ship I had earned £8 a month, less stoppages. It could take me two to three months to save the £10, depending on what it cost to live. With luck, there would be hotels needing waiters. That way, accommodation and food would be covered and I could save my wages.

The burning hot road went on and on, never seeming to get anywhere, the yellow dust whirling around and up in spirals every so often. One thing I knew for sure: I was going to need a hat in this country. My hankie was not very effective against this kind of sun; I was getting very red, and my mouth was so dry that my tongue was sticking to the roof of my mouth.

Eventually, buildings started to appear. My head was all woozy and I couldn't think clearly. It was almost six o'clock. The walk had taken me over three hours and there was still a way to go to reach the town centre.

A sandy coloured car pulled up ahead, beneath a Police sign. A middle aged couple and their daughter got out and went inside, with what looked like their shopping. My fear of capture evaporated. I decided to give myself up to this policeman, who looked so ordinary and family-ish. I was past caring; all thoughts of prison or working in a sugar cane field were forgotten. I knocked on the door, which the policeman's wife opened. 'Come in, come in, you look exhausted. Sandra, get a glass of water for this young man.' I downed the water in one, and Sandra laughed and bounced off to the kitchen for a refill. She was very pretty and her eyes smiled warmly and openly. As her father came to stand behind her, I blurted out my story.

'So, you're from Nottingham. Then you'd know Trent Bridge.' He was serious cricket fan and this piece of information seemed to work wonders. If I'd been the top cadet at the police academy I couldn't have done better in his eyes.

'The agents for BHP are here in Newcastle. If your ship is

leased to them for twenty months they'll soon sort matters out. What I'm going to do is put you in a hotel for tonight. BHP can pay and tomorrow morning you report to their offices. Is that fair?'

'Yes, sir.' I was too exhausted to figure it out. When he offered to drive me to the hotel I accepted gratefully.

The following morning I didn't want to charge any more to the agents, so I skipped breakfast and reported to their office at 9.30. This turned to be one of the biggest buildings in town, with marble floors and high mahogany counters I could barely see over. A brittle lady in black with a big hooked nose and a mean mouth took my name and disappeared into an inner sanctum.

She returned some five minutes later and gave me a right telling off – in fact her language was worse than I'd ever heard on the ship. Embarrassed, I looked around to see who else could hear her language. I'd never heard a lady speak that way before and I stopped hearing her words, though I continued to look at her, my mouth open in awe. Her face was getting redder, and her skin seemed to be separating from her skull underneath. She looked like a talking skull, covered with loose, painted flesh.

I couldn't hear anything – not even the sound of my feet fleeing from the horrible sight. I didn't stop running for about three blocks. She had terrified me more than the cook ever did. I couldn't understand how her face had appeared to change. (Later, I was told it was hallucination brought on by fear and shock).

I found the YMCA and booked in for two nights, leaving me less than two bob. It was time to find a job. Also, I knew I had to go back and face Dragon Breath again: I had promised the policeman I would report to BHP. As it happened, when I plucked up courage to go back to BHP, the anticipated confrontation didn't occur. Maybe it was her day off. Instead, quite a nice man with dandruff informed me they'd spoken to the ship, which was just coming up the coast. The coastguard tender would run me out to rejoin it. The skipper was willing to take me back, as my service record on board was excellent.

'No, thanks,' I said, quite sure of that point, and surprised at my own firm reply.

'Then you'll have to report to the Federation,' he said, obviously disappointed his problem were not to be resolved so easily. 'Here is their address. Maybe they can get you another ship. But I doubt it, without papers. Are you sure Joe? You did sign a contract and you're obliged to honour it.'

'No, sir, I'm sorry. I won't go back on that ship.'

My third night I slept on the cliffs where I should have spent the two previous nights. Now I had no money left all, and the beans on toast yesterday had been my last meal. Tomorrow I was going to need a more creative approach to eating. I had walked around the town for three days and now knew all the cafes, restaurants and hotels. There were no vacancies for a pommie waiter.

The morning started with the warm blue sky caressing the day into life – the sort of weather the holiday brochures portray, that never materialises. Yet here it seemed that cloudless blue skies were as common as buildings, cars and houses, and so not the same topic of conversation as I was used to. It was a good day to get a bit bold. I had to go to the Federation Office at 10am, which left me plenty of time to get some breakfast. I knew just where to go – in fact, I'd two meals there already, so I was almost a regular. This time, though, I was broke. I went in and sat down at the green, plastic-topped chrome table.

'Beans on toast is it again, sonny?'

'Yes please, and a mug of tea, thank you.' I was aware of a tremble in my voice and hope he hadn't noticed.

In no time at all I had eaten my fill. Now came the scary bit. I stood up and carried my plate to the counter. 'Excuse me sir, but could I please wash some dishes, as I've got no money?'

He just looked at me, not speaking, his big face motionless. I wondered if perhaps he had not heard me and maybe I should say it again.

Then he exploded; obviously I had broken one of his sacred tenets. 'Oh yes, oh yes, you'd like to wash some dishes! Well, let's see what we can find for you to do.' He took my arm and led me to the swinging door at the rear and into the kitchen.

It was awful – obviously his staff had left months ago. The place was piled high with pans and dishes, all congealing with meals cooked days ago, at least. Under it all, somewhere, was a sink.

'You'll think twice before you pull that little stunt again. You can go when this place is all cleaned up. You'll find some Vim and a scrubber under the sink.' He banged out into the front shop again. I wondered if there was a back door through which I could escape, but found that it had a big brass padlock on it.

It was gone two o'clock before I'd finished. His lunch trade kept adding to the pile, but finally I went out and said I was done. He led me back to the sink area. 'Not bad, kid. Are you hungry again?'

'Yes, sir,' I replied sullenly.

'Well, sit down and I'll fix you something.' And he did, two eggs and a pile of beans. 'Suppose you want tea with that?' he said sternly. I didn't answer, but he gave me one.

'Thank you, sir.'

'Well, you've done a good Job out there. You can come back tomorrow if you like.' I thought about that – no chance. He wasn't too bad: the fact that he never smiled made him appear fiercer than he was and he growled rather more than spoke, but I got the impression he didn't get on with people very easily.

By the time I reached the shipping office, it was gone 3pm and the superintendent was livid.

'You were supposed to be here at ten this morning,' he said in a quiet, menacing tone. 'We've decided to send you back to Sydney. You'll report every day to the shipping office, and you'll stay at the British Sailors' Home at the bottom of George Street' – and, seemingly without drawing breath – 'do you know we've had the police and everyone out looking for you. Where the hell have you been?'

'Working for a meal. It just took longer than I expected,' I replied, with justification.

'Well, you're not doing one of your disappearing acts again. The police will take you to the Sydney train, which leaves at six this evening. Till then, sit over there and don't move.'

The policeman soon arrived and took me to the station, where he bought me a cup of tea and a big, yellow cake, which went down a treat. He was quite young compared to everyone else I had been meeting, but he didn't seem very happy.

'Okay, let's go,' he said, taking my elbow and leading me towards the train.

'It's not five o'clock yet,' I protested. 'There's still an hour before it goes, and I'd prefer to wait in the tea room.'

'I know, but I'm off duty now and I've got to see you onto the train before I can go home.'

'Okay,' and so we boarded the train and looked for the guard. We found him in the rear carriage, which had no seats; it was for carrying parcel and mail. The policeman handcuffed my left wrist and sat me on the floor, clamping the other bracelet to a pipe near the rear corner of the compartment.

'Sorry about this kid, but they're my orders.' His eyes showed he was sorry, and he quickly turned away to the guard.

'These are his transit papers, this is the key. You are to release him to the police in Sydney. Don't lose him – he seems to have a habit of vanishing. He's under age so we're not prosecuting, but the shipping Federation feel he'll stand a better chance of getting a ship out from Sydney.'

The guard, it turned out, was not bad. He shared his sandwiches with me and made tea a couple of times. He told me of his lack of adventures as a young man, and what seemed a life of regret ever since. He also told me of his wife and two girls, who, it seemed, didn't really know or care for him.

We arrived in Sydney at ten minutes before midnight. A policeman removed my handcuffs and then took me to the Sailors' Home, telling me to report to the padre every day at the Flying Angel Mission to Seamen 100 yards up the road. I was shown to my room, which was little more than a cell. Alone at last, I looked around at the narrow bed, the two-drawer chest and the wooden chair. I lay back on the bed and looked up at the moon shinning through the bars of the window, wondering what delights awaited me in Sydney, and particularly, how easy or otherwise it would be to get a ship. I gingerly rubbed my left wrist, which was quite raw from the handcuffs, and wondered if the padre would have a first aid kit. I wrote in my diary: 'Arrived back in Sydney. Staying at the Sailors' Home, got my own room. Tomorrow will look for a ship home.' I must have fallen asleep then, because that's all I wrote, and in the morning I was lying, still dressed, on top of the covers, my diary on the floor.

At 6.30am I was called and given a mop and bucket to wash the floor of my room and the passage.

CHAPTER 16

Vindi Boy – Sydney

By 8am we had been given a breakfast and were put out on the street for the day. The other guest at the hostel was a man in his early thirties called Keith, who I'd met at breakfast. He'd jumped ship in Fiji, having succumbed to the charms of a local Indian girl. The way he explained it, she'd promised him a lifestyle he'd dreamt of, as she was the daughter of a wealthy sugar cane farmer. However, it seems her father had not been impressed and had him arrested and flown to Sydney in quick time.

'What are you going to do with your day, Joe? You know they won't let you back in here until five o'clock.'

'Well, I've got to report to the padre at the Mission, and go to the Federation at ten o'clock, then I thought I'd have a walk around the city. What are you going to do?'

'Well I've met this 'sheila' who works in a cafe at the top of George Street. She slips me some nosh if I go in when she's busy, then when she finishes at four we go for a walk in the park and I return the favour, like.' Keith leant back against the stone wall, drawing heavily on his cigarette. He obviously enjoyed his good looks and saw them as his ticket to an easier life.

'But haven't you found a job or a ship to join?' I asked.

Keith flicked away his butt and smiled. 'Well, I've got a mate who works at the Rex and he gets me the occasional few hours dish-washing if the regular guy doesn't show, but you'll find it's not easy. They don't like employing poms. Say, can I cadge another fag off you?'

'Sure, take the packet.' I gave him the remainder. I didn't smoke and only carried them as currency. Keith was my only friend here, so I wanted to show I had something he wanted, in return for his advice and friendship.

'As for a ship – yes, I've got that figured. On the third of February the 'Oronsay' comes in and I'm going home on that. There'll be plenty of jobs – you'll see.'

'But that's eight weeks away! How do you know you can get on it?' I queried.

'Oh, I will, you'll see. If you stick with me, kid, you'll get on it too. Look, I've got to go and meet my mate up the Cross. I'll see you at five.'

The Mission wasn't open, so I walked to the Federation building, which was just about to open.

The Superintendent didn't seem pleased to see me. 'You're a burden I don't need, and deserters, especially little pommie pricks who thought they could just walk ashore without papers, should be in prison. No matter your age, if you're old enough to commit a crime, you're old enough to do the time. Illegal entry to a country carries six months. Are you aware of that?'

'Yes, sir.'

The Superintendent was a big man, who had obviously spent time working hard – at sea I guessed. He stood behind his desk and towered over me, his big hands spread upon his desk. His wiry ginger hair was receding, his balding head covered with speckles and scabs. His yellowing eyes, looking at me, almost made me cringe.

'You are a responsibility I don't want, especially just before Christmas. Let me make it perfectly clear: I don't like deserters. Who the hell do you think you are? You will stay at the home until I say otherwise; if you go adrift again, we will have to lock you up. Is that clear?'

'Yes, sir.'

'You will walk the docks every day and go to every ship to find a passage. It doesn't have to be to England, it just has to be out of here – is that clear?'

'Yes, sir.'

'Not having papers, most captains won't welcome you. But there's always the chance that one will. You will report here every Friday and Monday morning with a list of the ships you've visited. I want the captain's name, or the first officer's. And I will check up

105

that you've actually been to the ship – is that clear?'

'Yes, sir.'

'Now get out of my sight, you little shit.'

I didn't need telling twice. I was out and down the street, heading for the Flying Angel. The mission stood on a small rise almost at the bottom of George Street. Most of the surrounding buildings were large warehouses servicing the docks. They looked dark and almost sinister. This was not the best end of town: the ' Rocks' was home ground to prostitutes, deadbeats and deserters, of which I was just one more. Its pubs were numerous, and none of them elegant. It was not an area to dawdle in.

The big, red-brick building of the Mission welcomed all seamen. The cleaning lady mopping the polished floor said the padre would be along at ten, and that I could pour myself a cuppa from the big, green metal teapot on the counter. She seemed so pleasant and cheerful. I wondered why people with authority were so often nasty with it.

The padre turned out to be great. Although he asked a lot of questions, he wasn't threatening. Unlike the Superintendent at the Federation, this man seemed quite pleased to have me under his wing. The Rev. Parr sat me down in his office and laid out the rules for my reporting to him, then added:

'You can have a cuppa anytime and some sandwiches at lunch time. In return, you can help Molly keep this place tidy. Molly will tell you what she wants done and there's always some dishes to do. Have you written to your mother since you arrived?'

'No, sir. I didn't want her to worry.'

'Well, don't you think she'll worry more, not knowing where you are? Now promise me you'll write. I'll give you a card, so there's no excuse.' And so saying, he handed me a postcard of the Harbour Bridge. 'It doesn't have to say much. Just let her know you're okay.' I wondered if these padres owned shares in postcard companies. I didn't write, even though the Rev. Parr continued to encourage me. But my mum wouldn't know that I was adrift if I didn't tell her, so better I arrive home early and surprise her. Or wait till I had a ship at least. That seemed reasonable.

Every morning I would dutifully set out around the docks. The newspaper at the mission told of all the shipping movements. Mostly this meant walking around the Rocks and over the Pyrmont Bridge then through the cement works to the far docks and, in the afternoon, over to Woolloomooloo. This was quite a trek and the December heat made the pavements hot to walk on. I soon learned to hug the shade from the warehouses. It took all day to cover all the docks and it was disheartening, because the answer was always the same: without my seaman's book I wasn't welcome. On one occasion a small freighter bound for Hamburg almost took me on, but some union busy-body came and made sure I didn't get the job. I told the Superintendent, but he simply said, 'What do you expect? Why should you get a job before a paid up member?'

On one occasion I managed to get a job for the Coca-Cola bottling company, but on returning after lunch was told by the foreman, 'The union wants you out. I'm sorry; the job must go to a union member,' and he gave me half a crown, which I'm sure came from his own pocket. The power of the unions was quite amazing. I belong to the Seamen's Union, as a requirement to get a ship. Now I was on the outside. I wondered who the unions represented. It seemed only themselves, but that was probably my view simply because it was the union stopping me getting a ship or a job. I knew they were against the employers. It didn't feel right and I obviously didn't understand. To me, they were just another big authority which threatened individuals like me. I didn't try to find work again. It was enough traipsing round the docks every day.

The padre had me helping him put up a few decorations in the mission, and he produced a small tree. I wasn't sure that it was a real Christmas tree, but it was a fir tree and fun to tie the glass decorations on.

Christmas for me had always seemed a lonely time, a period designed for the benefit of others – those who had families. It had an air of exclusion which was accompanied by disappointments and drunken arguments, yet here it was quite different. I was glad to help the padre with something that was obviously important to him. His energy and enthusiasm were contagious – he was determined all sailors who came to the mission could at least feel, as he put it, the spirit of Christmas.

It seemed there were two worlds: one that looked forward to the festive season and thoroughly enjoy it, and the real world, which saw it as an annual commercial success that turned up the volume on loneliness and poverty. I must admit the traditional Christmas story had never seemed more than an unlikely take to me. However, the generous and caring nature of the padre did show that people have a good side. Maybe this was the season to try to find it. Come to think of it, though, there were some I'd met who definitely didn't have one and no amount of carols and Christmas trees were going to find it. The padre, though, was determined to lift those that came through his door out of the dark abyss and into his Christmas sunshine. If you were willing to sing a few carols, there was a Christmas dinner at no charge, with pudding and even crackers to pull. I felt sure the dinner and trimmings all came out of his pocket, and there was a sudden surge of souls claiming to be seamen. He turned no one away and everyone received a present – admittedly simple, but at least something. I got some writing paper and six envelopes. Keith got a pen with the Sydney Harbour Bridge inside that snowed when shaken. He laughed and said, 'Snow in this town, wishful bloody thinking. You could fry eggs on the pavement.' The padre heard him, but it did nothing to dent his benevolent smile. He was in his element and everyone appreciated his effort.

I spent most of the day helping in the kitchen, doing the endless stream of dishes and making pots of tea. It saved me having to walk endlessly around the docks outside. Today I was part of what was happening, eating cakes and sarnies all day. It really was a magical Xmas.

The weeks passed slowly, but finally it was the third of February. Keith was very excited. He and I set off at 7.30am to try the 'Oronsay', which was over in Pyrmont.

We climbed the long, covered gangway and Keith said, 'See you later, kid.' I made my way to the purser's office to tell my story. I guess Keith had so convinced me I'd get a job that when I was escorted off by a master-at-arms I was surprised and crestfallen. I'd counted the days till the 'Oronsay' arrived to take me home, fully believing I would be leaving Sydney today.

I made my way back to the Mission, feeling frustrated. If, after seven weeks, I still couldn't get a ship without a 'book', then I was wasting my time looking every day. I thought, if Keith leaves today I'll be on my own, and I can't get a job without a work permit. If I'm still here by the end of April, I'll turn sixteen and be old enough for a prison sentence. So I've got to stow away on a ship, or move out of the city to where the unions have less control. I wondered if Salty was still up in those hills. I liked him, but I had no way of getting up there and he would most likely be long gone by now. By the time I reached the Mission I was as though a cloud had descended upon my life. I couldn't see a way ahead.

Rev. Parr came rushing out of his office to greet me. 'Oh Joe, there you are. You've to report to the Federation immediately,' he said, as though off-loading a message he didn't relish.

'What for? It's only Tuesday. I'm not due to check in till Friday,' I replied.

'No, it's something else. The Superintendent said you were to come up the moment you came in.' He was very insistent.

'Can I have a cuppa first?' I said, still reeling from this morning's rejection on the much awaited 'Oronsay'. The prospect of seeing Thunderguts at the shipping office and having to withstand one of his blasts of 'Is that absolutely clear boy?' was not something I looked forward to.

'Of course you can,' said the padre. 'You look as though you could do with something to eat as well.' He steered me over to Molly, who was busy chopping carrots. 'Give our young hero some sustenance, please Molly.'

I gratefully downed a piece of cake and a cup of tea, which made me feel much better. I hurried up to Thunderguts' office at the Federation. The secretary, who knew me by sight by now, said, 'Go on in, son,' so I took a deep breath and opened the door.

'Right, you little toe-rag, Interpol are after you. It seems your mother became worried when her allowance stopped. She learned from the shipping company that you had jumped ship in Sydney, and got on to Interpol. I take it you never even wrote to her, did you?'

'No sir, I didn't want to worry her.'

'Don't give me that crap,' he boomed.

'Well you're being shipped home DBS on the 'Oronsay' today, which means you will work your passage back and be paid a token shilling when you get off, which is probably more than you're worth.'

'But sir, I went down to the 'Oronsay' this morning, and there's no jobs: they were quite definite. In fact, they had the master-at-arms escort me ashore.'

Thunderguts' eyes bulged and the veins in his red necks stood out. 'Don't you argue with me, you little shit. The British Consul has arranged your passage as a laundry boy. Here is the instruction: don't lose it. And here is your seaman's book that's arrived from your old ship. Now, get out of my sight.'

I didn't need telling twice. I gratefully took my book and the envelope containing the instructions, and left his office. Outside, his secretary gave me a big smile and wished me good luck. I wished her good luck too, at which she looked a little puzzled, but still smiled. Had I been a bit older I might have realised that, far from fearing her boss as I did, she probably thought he was very manly and appealing.

The Sailors' Home was still locked, but I had only a pair of pants and a shirt there. I didn't need them. I called at the Mission to say good bye to the padre and Molly. Molly was busily serving lunches and waved me to grab a plate and fill up. When she served me she was smiling like she'd known all along, but asked, 'So how was Dragon Breath, Joe?'

'Oh great. He's got me on the 'Oronsay' and I'm joining today – and he gave me my book.'

'You mean he's had your book all this time, over two months, and made you tramp round all the docks every day. That doesn't sound very fair. He's been punishing you himself. Never mind, Joe. You've got your ship now. I bet you're happy!'

'Yeah, it's a smashing ship. One like I always dreamt of going on.'

'Well, you get that lunch down you and make sure you see the padre before you go.'

I was starving. All the excitement of the morning had given me a good appetite. Molly came over with a big jam donut.

'Here you are, can you manage this as well? We're going to miss you around the place, Joe.'

'Thanks, Molly. You look after me like a mum.' She smiled and disappeared into the kitchen. When I'd finished I took my plates back, then quickly gathered up the others from the tables and took them through to wash.

'No, you don't' said Molly, coming through from the kitchen.

'You've got a ship to Join, now get off with you. Heh, don't I get a hug?'

I gave her a big hug and felt choked. I'd like to have hugged her longer but she pushed me away. 'Get out of here now! Go and see the padre.'

Just as I was going to knock on his door, it opened. 'Ah Joe, come in. Are you all ready to go?'

'Yes, sir. Thank you for your kindness to me, and Molly, of course.'

'Don't you worry – I will pass on your thanks. She's a wonderful woman that, and she's not had an easy life, though she'd be the last to tell you. Now your run along and be glad your mother got on to the authorities to find you.'

'Yes, sir.'

'Well, it's been a pleasure having you help us out.' He held his hand out. The formality of shaking hands didn't change the feeling of goodwill.

'Good luck, Joe.'

'Thank you, sir.'

I ran most of the way back to Pyrmont and bounded breathlessly up the gangway again, clutching my authority. It was a pleasure to return to the stuffy officers behind the desk at the purser's office and present it with a smile. The assistant purser, a tall woman in her thirties with a starched white uniform that made her look like a nurse, read the note and looked unhappy. Clearly trying to avoid the responsibility, she made several telephone calls and spoke to unseen authorities. In the end she said, 'You don't belong up here. Go and sit over there. The assistant laundryman will be up shortly.' Then she turned away to talk to a passenger.

I looked around at all the fancy fittings, the rich woodwork, the fresh paintwork and the high polish, and felt happy. A few months ago, when I saw her sister ship the 'Orcades', I never dreamt I'd be sailing on a ship like this quite so soon. I was glad I hadn't written to my mum!

'Hello, you must be Joe,' said a foreign-sounding voice just behind me.

111

'Yes,' I said, standing up to shake the outstretched hand.

'Hi. I'm Toni, the second laundryman.' Toni was no taller than me, with olive skin, black hair and moustache, and darting brown eyes.

'Come on. I'll take you to your cabin. Have you any luggage?' he said.

'No, I haven't needed much.'

After descending at least four deck levels we came out on a wide passage. 'This is the crew deck and main working alleyway; we're at the end here.' It was quite busy. As we walked, we passed a cabin lit with coloured lights, bras and knickers hanging on lines to dry. Several well-dressed ladies passed us and most seemed to have a smile for Toni. One, wearing a wide-brimmed hat, tight dress, high heels and carrying a cigarette in a long holder, put her hand on his shoulder. 'Antonio, darling, will I see you later?'

'C'mon Rachel, you'll get me a bad name,' he said, brushing past.

'You can bring your new friend if you like,' she called.

'Just ignore her,' Toni said as he led the way to a side alley and opened the door of a huge cabin. Five pairs of bunks were separated by two narrow tin wardrobes. There were lockers, but no chests of drawers; no furniture at all apart from the bunks, and each one had a tiny ten-by-five inch locker, about two inches deep, on the bulkhead. This little locker, it transpired, was each man's private zone which, in a ten-berth cabin, was rated highly.

'There you are: that's your bunk up there, and this fat slob scratching himself is Chas.'

'Yeah hi, juwanna beer?' offered Chas by way of welcome.

'No thanks, not yet,' I said, feeling still unsure of myself on this new territory and what might lie ahead this day.

'It's not so big when all ten of us are home at the same time,' added Chas. 'Think yourself lucky it's not a fourteen-berther.'

Toni opened the door. 'C'mon, I'll show you the mess. There'll be tea on down there. I expect you could do with something to eat.'

I was getting more food today than at any time during the last three months (except Christmas day), and that suited me. 'Yes, I'm starving,' and I was. The run over to the ship must have shaken down Molly's pie and mashed potatoes.

* * *

CHAPTER 17

At Sea Again

The mess was huge, with a servery down one side and row upon row of long tables and chairs filling the room.

'There's usually tea and coffee available in here,' said Toni over his shoulder as he started putting cups and plates on a tray. I followed and we finished up with two platefuls of sandwiches, some tabnabs and cups of tea.

'You can draw a mug from stores and keep it with you. That way you'll be able to take your tea or coffee back to the cabin.'

We found a seat next to three other men wearing T-shirts and jeans.

'This is Joe. He's just joining today and will be working with us in the sweat box. He's going back DBS, so any help you can give him I'm sure will be welcome.'

They all said hello and told me their names, which I promptly forgot, and followed with a barrage of questions: 'Did you jump ship? – Where? What ship? What made you jump?'

'Okay, you guys, give him a break,' chimed in Toni, coming to the rescue.

'They're all right really, just like to gossip,' he filled up with another sandwich. 'There's nine of us in the laundry, plus you,' he went on with his mouth full. 'These three robbers and Chas you met in the cabin. The boss and Reggie are ashore this afternoon, and I don't know where Jordie and Davey are.'

'How many crew are there altogether?' I asked Toni.

'Well your crew number is 579, so that's probably it,' he replied.

'Cor – my last ship only carried thirty-four.'

'What was your Job?' asked Pete, lighting up two cigarettes and passing one to Mickey.

'I was cabin boy – it was my first trip, but I always dreamt of working on a big liner like this. It's so different. Not only the boat, of course, but you all seem so friendly.'

'That doesn't mean there are no fights,' put in Gerry. 'Though usually that's some queer in a jealous rage. In the sweat box we're all straight – I think!'

They all laughed and we went back to the cabin.

'If any of you want to go ashore, remember we sail at nine tonight, so back on board by eight,' Toni reminded us.

'Okay,' said Chas, putting down his Hank Jansen Novel.

'Who's for a few bevvies up the Rex?'

'Yeah, why not,' Pete sighed. 'Come on, Mick, we can have a laugh.'

Mickey, pulling his T-shirt over his head, said: 'Yer on. Are you coming Joe?'

'No thanks, I'm quite glad to be on board and I've seen quite enough of Sydney.'

'God, you lot are thick,' said Toni. 'The lad's got no money, you're just embarrassing him.'

'No, no, it's all right, honest,' I protested, more concerned at not losing the new job that luck had just presented me.

'You're coming with us kid and no bloody argument, isn't that right, lads?' said Pete with an air of authority in his heavy Newcastle accent.

'Yeah, sure,' added Mickey, 'Of course. Let's go. And if any of these cowboys give you any cheek, you tell me – okay?' I smiled and didn't know what to say. Their good humour and generosity was somewhat overwhelming. I was so happy.

Mickey finished doing up his fresh shirt. 'Cat got your tongue, Joe? We'd like you to come with us, honest. Look, you're going to be doing the same work as us – without pay. The least we can do is buy you a beer – okay?'

'Yes, okay. Thank you.' I felt a strong surge of emotion and ducked out of the cabin to find the carsie before they saw my eyes red and watery. I rinsed my face in cold water and went back to the cabin smiling.

'Okay, let's go,' Mickey ordered, sounding like a cavalry platoon leader, which was strange. He wasn't very big and had a Liverpool twang, yet he had a quiet air of authority. We bundled off ashore and into a taxi waiting on the wharf.

Mick and I squeezed in the front and the other three in the back. Toni had to remain on board while the chief laundryman was ashore even though the laundry closed at midday in port.

We went over to the Rex Hotel. It was T-bone steaks and chips all round, and my coke had been liberally weakened with rum. The other drank beer as though Australia was about to run out of it at any moment.

Two girls had Joining the party and Pete asked them, 'Why are all your cars painted that sandy colour?'

'Because you Brits kept all the black paint for yours!' the short brunette replied. It was a question that she'd obviously heard before. We all laughed, and enjoy these girls' ability to give as good as they got.

'Okay,' Pete countered. 'How come you've only got one bloody tree, the eucalyptus?!'

'There's lots of different types of eucalyptus and our koalas don't think much of your stuffy old oak trees. Anyway, they wouldn't last five minutes out here. Your trees like it cold and wet!'

'She's got you there, mate.' observed Chas.

This happy banter went on and became more raucous until almost eight o'clock, when Jordie and Mickey bundled us outside and into a cab.

'Did you get her address?' asked Pete of Chas, who had become much more forward with a few beers inside him.

'Yes, of course – both of them! I don't waste time. Next trip I'll be right in there! You'll see.'

'Five bob says you never get a letter,' Pete challenged.

'You're on, sucker,' Chas replied. 'You're all witnesses now!'

We piled out of the cab at the wharf and I looked up at the huge liner. It was ablaze with lights and throngs of passengers lining the rails, shouting last minute endearments to friends and relatives on the wharf. Coloured streamers cascaded down to outstretched arms and upturned faces, some with tears, some with smiles.

We made our way through and boarded via the crew gangway, which was almost at wharf level and led straight on to the working alleyway.

'Can we see her sail?' I asked Mickey.

'Sure, from the well deck,' he said, as he moved away from Pete, who had been steering him. 'But I'm too pissed. You'll have to find someone else to show you how to get there.'

'Joe, I'll take you,' Toni's voice sounded from behind his bunk curtains. His light went on. He swung his legs out and dropped to the deck. He was obviously not quite awake yet.

'You lot are like a herd of bloody elephants! How can I sleep? What time is it?' he said, putting on his jeans.

'Twenty to nine by my Samuel Everite,' boomed Chas. The band will be playing "Now Is The Hour". I'm coming with you.' And so we wound our way up towards the bow.

The well deck was just abaft the fo'c's'l and the crew pub, known as the Pig, which led out on to it. However, it was always closed in port, so the majority on the deck were sober – or at least not far off. The band was playing 'When the Saints Come Marching In', and there was a festival air, balloons and streamers pouring unendingly from the passenger decks to the upturned faces on the wharf.

'Wow, that's amazing! How many do you reckon are down there?' I asked Toni.

'At least a thousand, I should think. There's over twelve hundred passengers, so there's probably as many folk seeing them off. It was wonderful. Though none were waving me off, I felt the celebration very moving. In fact, it was the most impressive sight I could recall; it was absolutely magical.

A cheer rose up as the ship started to edge silently away from the wharf, the black knife of water slowly widening. The band played 'Now Is the Hour'. The streamers stretched taut until that last connection finally snapped and we were completely free. The whistles died and the last few lone balloons drifted skyward, their colours caught briefly in the ship's glow as they rose and disappeared into the dark night.

As our bow came around and we turned towards the huge Sydney Harbour Bridge, the crowds started to disappear, the emotional ones lingering to see the ship away into the night. The tugs released our lines. The ship's horn blasted three times to bid final farewell to the now unrecognisable faces still staring out into the harbour. On board, a few passengers remained on deck as the lights of Sydney passed our starboard side. We quietly glided under the bridge. I knew Molly and the padre would wave into the darkness from the rear window of the Mission and I felt a hot tear run down my cheek.

The Pig was open, and more serious matters required the attention of my new friends.

'C'mon Joe, let's get some bevvies and see if the crown and anchor board will pay.'

I quickly wiped my eyes with my sleeve and went to join them. Most of the tables were already full, and the crown and anchor board was already running. I watched fascinated at the amount of money passing, it made the gambling on the 'Princess Tara' seem very passive. A steward in full whites had three bets in a row and each time lost a big white fiver. It was a lot of money to lose so quickly, yet he didn't seem to all bothered. I decided he'd just paid for my education. Toni and Chas were only betting in two shilling pieces, Toni doubling up each time. 'That's it,' he declared. 'Twelve shillings, - that'll do,' and he pushed through to the bar for another round of drinks.

'I don't know how you do it?' moaned Chas, 'You always bloody win.'

'Because I know when to stop. You're too greedy. You've always got to try just one more time, haven't you? You can't help yourself,' said Toni in a voice that sounded fed up at repeating the same message.

I drank my Coke. I was in heaven.

* * *

CHAPTER 18

Melbourne

The following day we turned to at 8am and worked through till five. I'd never seen so many sheets in my life. Mickey, Pete, Chas and I worked the big colander, a huge rotating drum into which Mickey and Pete fed wet sheets. They came through the press hot, dry and well-starched, ready for me and Chas to fold on the other side. The speed of the drum was slowed down so that I could get the precision timing of the folding right and work in unison not only with Chas, but also with Mickey and Pete feeding them in. It took about an hour for me to make a few mistakes and learn to work in the system as a part of a team, but soon the machine was picking up speed, and by lunch time we were working quite hard. My arms felt like lead and my fingers were red from the hot fabric, but I was happy, the cheerful atmosphere like a tonic. I thought this must be what belonging to a family is like and I worked keenly to match the others' output.

However, by knocking off time at 5pm I was stuffed. Being on my feet, concentrating all day was something new to adapt to, but that was okay. In a way, it was fun, and as I collapsed on my bunk, I decided that being part of the team was worth more than the wages I wasn't getting.

Later we showered and headed down to the mess. Rachel was there, though not all dressed up in her finery as I'd seen her yesterday. I really had thought she was part of the female crew, but even on liners the only females were either purser's office staff or nurses from the hospital on board. All the rest of the crew were male and about seventy per cent of those were gay, some of whom were very convincing as females. Rachel was one of these. Today she wore a white T-shirt and tight pink shorts and flip-flops. Her face literally lit up when she saw Toni, though she said nothing as we passed by the table where she was sitting to join the food queue.

I recalled Gerry's comment of yesterday about us all being

straight in the laundry, and decided to let Rachel's unguarded smile pass as if unnoticed. Obviously Toni preferred discretion. I soon discovered the ship was a huge gossip shop anyway, so perhaps I was mistaken.

We sat together, all nine of us. The chief laundryman ate in the leading hands' mess. Actually, Toni could have eaten there too, but he said 'How would I know what you toe-rags were up to if I ate up there?' I couldn't help thinking that might not be the only reason.

'Hey, Joe, you're coming with us in Melbourne. We're going to see Chas's sister, isn't that right, Chas?'

'Oh yeah, she might have a young friend for you, Joe.'

'Well, I'd like to come with you, but I'm not sure about her girl friend. She might be fifteen stone,' I said bravely.

'Oh well, maybe she'll have more than one friend and you can choose.'

They all laughed, obviously having met Chas's sister. It was starting to sound like a set-up. A deep voice behind me said, 'Are you wicked boys trying to lead this young body astray?'

I turned to see a tall man with very masculine features, who smiled down at me and held out his hand. 'Hello I'm Laurie, and you are?'

'Joe,' I said, not sure whether to stand. 'Joseph Lawson. I joined yesterday in Sydney.'

'And you obviously work in the sweat box with these lovely young men?'

I didn't know quite what to say – 'Yes, sir.'

'Oh please, don't insult me!' Laurie, or Big Laurie as she was known, was very theatrical, and though a long way from petite, was, for all that, feminine in the Monroe style.

'Laurie always likes to look after the young,' said Chas. 'It brings out her mothering instincts!'

'Well, dear, someone's got to protect them from you horny young men, and if you're planning on leading Joe astray tomorrow you can forget it. Joe, tomorrow you'll come ashore with me and let these randy layabouts get spotty dicks on their own. I'll call for you at two o'clock.' With that she left the mess.

Toni came to my rescue as the lads teased me. 'Don't worry, Joe. Big Laurie will look after you and god help anyone who tries to lay a hand on you. She's very possessive.'

'But I don't want to sleep with Laurie,' I protested. It was really a question.

'Oh, don't worry. Laurie won't touch you,' said Toni, 'and maybe, after all, you're a bit young for Chas's sister!'

They all laughed. Peter said, 'Tell you one thing, Joe, if any others try to take you under their wing, you'd better let them know Laurie's your mother. Otherwise there could be some harsh words, to put it mildly.'

The following day we closed the laundry at one o'clock and downed a quick lunch before getting ready to go ashore. Laurie came to the cabin promptly at two and, seeing me in my new jeans and T-shirt, of which I was quite proud, said, 'You don't seriously expect to come ashore with me looking like that do you, Joe?' and handed me a blue shirt and button-down collars made of sea island cotton. 'At least put that on, and hurry.'

The shirt was really great and I felt extra special in it. 'Thank you, Laurie. Can I keep it?'

'Yes, of course. I bought it in 'Frisco but it's too small for me, and it looks better on you. Now, come on. We have a car waiting.'

'Who's "we"? Is someone else coming?' I asked.

'Yes, sister Rachel at least, and maybe Gretchen,' said Laurie.

Sure enough, there on the wharf was Rachel and a tall blond man whose yellow trousers were so tight-fitting they looked like they'd been painted on. He wore an equally tight cream silk shirt.

'Gretchen, say hello to Joe. He's my new protégé and works with Rachel's lovely fella in the sweat box.'

'Hi Joe. Nice to have you with us. Laurie always has good taste.'

'Which is more than you, darling. How many times do I have to tell you about the yellow trousers? They just don't go with your blond looks,' Laurie said as we piled into the cab. 'Such lovely lallies, but the colour's dreadful. Why don't you give them to Rachel? Her brunette colouring would suit them better.' Rachel smiled appreciatively at the thought of possessing these obviously very expensive pants.

'You can dream, honey,' countered Gretchen. 'I had these specially made in Italy and they wouldn't fit your big hips.'

'Now, now, girls, stop squabbling. Driver, the Windsor please.'

The limo taxi noiselessly left the dock behind and we drove up town to the top of Collins Street, to what I had no doubt was the best hotel in Melbourne. My three companions strode in as though they owned the place. The beautiful woodwork and furnishings created an air of serene opulence. To me it felt almost sacred, rather like a cathedral, where conversations were discreet – almost whispered – and where in a cathedral the mitred bishop silently moved around as though on wheels, here the staff moved light-footed about duties in this temple of the material world. It was simply grand.

Heads turned, pin-stripe suits and broderie anglaise fell silent in discreet mid-sentence to witness the young men who had invaded their temple, whose gay casual clothes, obviously expensively tailored, did nothing to hide their mincing glide across the vast room and up the grand staircase to the private bar.

'Pay no attention, they're just jealous,' whispered Laurie.

The afternoon passed all too quickly. We went shopping in a nearby arcade, where Laurie bought me a pair of slacks and Rachel and Gretchen bought themselves slacks and shirts. They seemed to be known everywhere we went. After our shopping spree we returned to the grill at the Windsor and had a feast of huge prawns followed by strawberries in a chocolate and brandy sauce. I was so happy and felt safe, a luxury I'd almost forgotten. I couldn't help feeling there was a piper to pay somewhere, but I pushed down that little nagging thought, determined to enjoy the treat.

'It's really good of you, Laurie, to bring me with you. It's been magic, and a long way from working all day for a plate of beans.'

'That's quite all right, Joe, it's our pleasure. Though we do have to have an understanding, is that okay?'

'Yes Laurie, what?' – thinking, here it comes.

'Well, as you know, young ladies always like to talk about their boy friends – or other people's boy friends. Sometimes it's skite, sometimes real. Well, we need to feel safe that you won't go running off to tell your cabin mates what we discuss. Now that's fair, isn't it?' Laurie dabbed her mouth with the napkin and looked right at me. I saw the smile, but felt the eyes that held me were, just for that moment, hard and very definite. There had been no threat, yet I understood perfectly.

I wouldn't tell anyone – honest,' I protested enthusiastically. Laurie's large mouth smiled even wider and Rachel looked positively relieved.

Gretchen beckoned the waiter with a raised eyebrow and pursed lips. He brought the bill in leather wallet on a silver tray. She looked at the bottom line and peeled a pile of notes on to the tray.

'That's all right dear,' she said quietly to the waiter and he disappeared to discover discreetly how much Gretchen had tipped him. He knew how generous these three queens were, and he wasn't disappointed. He reappeared to bid us farewell and urged us to hurry back.

As if by magic, by the time we reached the foyer our limo was waiting for us, its doors open. Rachel slipped some money to the concierge and we left with them repeating, 'We look forward to your next visit.'

The city lights were now on as we sped back to the ship, and as we entered the dock gates we passed four of the crew loudly singing their way back home, staggering with arms on shoulders like a drunken eight-legged beast. The contrast to our elegant passage was not lost on me and I wholeheartedly voted for luxury.

* * *

CHAPTER 19

Wheeling and Dealing

The only person in our cabin who did not work in the laundry was Paddy, who hailed from Belfast and worked as a utility steward, which simply meant he worked in the U Gang washing dishes, fetching stores every day from the hold to feed 2000 people, and doing the most menial Jobs on the ship. Like ours, his uniform consisted simply of jeans and white T-shirt, but unlike us he had to work during meal times, as he had a snooze each afternoon while we worked, and he had to work most nights.

To work on the U Gang meant that you couldn't handle the responsibility of being a winger (table steward) or a BR [bedroom steward], both of which entailed not only skill and hard work, but an ability to handle passengers with all their idiosyncrasies, which, on long sea voyages, tended to come to the surface after the first couple of weeks at sea. The passenger, of course, is always right, no matter how arrogant or unreasonable their demands. A winger who forgets this for one second could easily find himself on the U Gang. In Paddy's case, however, it was simply considered that his aspirations went no higher, and he seemed perfectly happy processing thousands of dishes every day. To say that the others in the cabin didn't think he was very bright was probably accurate, but they included him in rounds of drinks, let him sit with us in the mess and so on. But he was definitely not considered a thinker – perhaps more a piece of furniture which you saw every day but didn't get too excited about.

Anyway, he was always there – so when the conversation one evening became more involved, Paddy was there, but no one paid him any heed. Certainly it was not necessary to whisper secretively. During such evenings, the discussions in the cabin or the Pig, accompanies by a few bevvies, covered all subjects from gossip on board to politics, religion, sex and future goals of individuals. On this occasion Mickey, embarrassed by Liverpool's scoring in the league, wanted to change the subject from football, especially as Pete and Reggie's Newcastle United was responsible for the latest thrashing.

'You do realise the last sub is tomorrow – before Fremantle, that is.'

'Well, there's no women in Fremantle and it's all wogs after that,' answered Chas.

'Oh, that's great, isn't it? Your mind's always below your belt. Now, if you'd all shut up,' retorted Mickey. 'I'll tell you how we make a couple of bob. Who's game?'

Reggie replied, 'You can count me out if it's another of your money-making schemes. Beryl will kill me if she doesn't get a full wage packet when I get home.'

'Oh shut up, will you,' chimed Pete, 'let's hear Mickey out.'

'Okay, well, we each sub five pounds worth of cigarettes and stow them in our locker till Naples. There's guy comes on who'll buy them for the local black market. He buys heaps, and pays high prices. You'll get at least fifteen pounds back, but he only buys them in suitcase lots of fifty cartons. We could easily put up one case between us.'

Dave's attention was now enthralled, his cheeky East End attitude always ready to 'turn a sov', as he put it. 'Gentlemen, you insult lady luck. We should be in for at least four cases between us, if this is as good as slippery Mickey makes out. Wotcha say?'

Toni brought a measure of restraint to the discussion by suggesting we might not each have £20, 'And you're sure to want some spending money for Colombo and Naples at least'.

Tell you what,' said Mickey, 'each get what you're good for; it doesn't all have to be the same, and Toni can keep book on it.'

'Oh, no, you don't,' retorted Toni, opening another beer. 'Your scheme, you keep the book. I don't want to end up in the U Gang.'

'Are we agreed then, in units of givers,' said Mickey looking at each in turn.

'Pete?'

'Yes, okay.'

'Toni?'

'Yes.'

'Chas?'

'Of course, you don't think I'd miss out.'

'Dave?'

'Yeh, I'm in.'

'Gerry?'

'Yes, but I know I've only got one fiver.'

'Paddy?'

'Sure, it sounds too good to miss.'

'Right then, tomorrow night bring me your fags – no hang on: I couldn't store them all,' said Mickey, thinking aloud. 'You'll have to keep your own until we get to Naples. Just show me them and I'll enter you for whatever you've got, okay?'

The following night some long faces reported to Mickey that in fact they hadn't enough spare money to buy into the scheme, but that they'd do it next trip – and it was a great idea.

* * *

CHAPTER 20

The Indian Ocean

The long, rolling swell of the Indian Ocean gave us six days at sea without the disturbances of port changes. The routine was comfortable, though it was getting hotter each day.

It was across this stretch of ocean that the crew held their "Sods' Opera", and much excitement was building as it approached. It was the entertainment highlight of the trip and reputations were at stake in the theatrical atmosphere on board. Laurie, who was a barman in the first class lounge bar and therefore working till late during the evenings, was usually around at tea time, having spent much of the afternoon gossiping with her friends either on the well deck or in the mess. However, we had seen little of her since leaving Fremantle until today, the day of the performance.

'Hello, Joe,' she said, coming up behind me in the mess queue. 'Are you coming to the show tonight?'

'Yes, of course,' I replied, 'from all accounts it is very good.' I didn't really know much about it, but I wanted to support.

'Oh, good. You will sit at the front, won't you? You'll have to get there early. I shall be looking for you, though to be honest you can't see much over those lights.'

'When will you be on, Laurie?' I asked, putting some dessert on my tray and turning to go over and sit down.

Laurie followed me over. 'Well, I'm not sure. That bitch Georgina from the pool bar is doing favours for the assistant purser. Honestly, there's nothing she won't stoop to. It makes me sick. The assistant purser has overall authority over the entertainment officer, the band and all that glitters, but the laugh is she doesn't seem to realise that Georgina's one of us! She calls him Georgie Pie. Huh!'

* * *

Chas, Pete and Mickey were already eating and heard the last titbit as we found our seats. Chas, always with an ear for gossip, chortled. 'Are you saying, Laurie, that Georgina's giving the AP one?'

'It's not what I'm saying, you lovely boy; it's what the whole ship's talking about. What I do wonder is why no one has whispered in the AP's "shell-like".'

'Maybe they have,' said Pete, 'but maybe she thinks she can change Georgina's ways, save him, as it were.'

'Why is it,' Laurie asked 'that some women think a handsome man is wasted if he doesn't fancy women?'

'Well,' said Mickey, 'it seems this one does fancy the odd woman, now and again.'

'Huh. Odd is the right word for the AP,' said Laurie, 'she's so butch. I thought her tastes were more for young Purserettes.'

'Well,' said Mickey, 'like Georgina she probably has a taste for both fruits.'

'The whole point is that Georgina is getting to do her number as the finale, and is trying her damnedest to force me on first as a crowd warmer, if you please.'

'Well, is that so bad?' asked Chas.

Laurie didn't answer. Instead she just glared at Chas, no additional words necessary. After a few moments she tapped my thigh and excused herself. 'I'd better go and finish my frock, dear,' and so saying she left the mess.

Mickey put his arm around Chas. 'That's one young lady you've not impressed with your secret charm.'

The others laughed and, at Pete's suggestion of a beer, we all headed for the Pig to put away a couple before the show at 8pm.

We had just sat down with our drinks when someone's hand covered my eyes from behind and a voice whispered in my ear, 'I don't like little pommie pricks. Do I make myself perfectly clear?'

His hand let go and I swung around to see Keith, large as life.

'Give us a fag, kid!' he joked.

'What are you doing?' I asked. This was the first time I had seen Keith since the day we joining in Sydney.

'Tourist BR, but it's okay. At least I'm getting paid. I heard you were DBS,' he asked, 'Is that right?'

'Yes, Laundry boy, but these guys are great. This is Pete, Chas and Mickey. Keith and I shared the Sailors' Home in Sydney for quite some time. Hey, it's good to see you Keith. Are you going to the show?'

'The Sod's Opera? Nah, it's not for me. I like real women – you know that. As a matter of fact there's a solo mum in my section who's grateful for additional service while her young teenager is out pulling the young cadets. By the way Joe, a bit of news for you. When I was in Fremantle I was talking to the barman at the Victoria Hotel. He said they'd just fired a guy who was second steward on that ship of yours – the "Princess Tara" wasn't it? Hey, anyway, apparently there were twelve crews who jumped in Sydney and three of them had been caught. I guess one of them is you.'

'Why did they fire the Second?' I asked, not sorry to hear the news.

'Apparently so the story goes, he played some dirty cards and a big Aussie wiped the bar with him,' said Keith. 'Look kid, I've got to go. Look after yourself,' and he disappeared, clutching his beers.

That was the only time I ever saw Keith after Sydney. It struck me as strange that people could share such experiences and then not see each other again, but then I suppose all my life to date it had been no different. I had to learn to enjoy people as they come along, knowing that they would pass by.

'He's a bit of a character,' said Mickey, interrupting my musing.

'Yes, he's okay, is Keith. He jumped in Fiji – for the love of a good woman of course, only her dad had other plans for his daughter, so Keith was booted out on the first plane. I always thought of him as a bit of a swashbuckling pirate. He'd have been happy serving with Henry Morgan.'

'Well, c'mon,' said Chas, 'if we're going to the show we'd better get a move on.' He emptied his pot mug and fastened it back on his belt.

We arrived at twenty to eight and already the cinema was half full. Once a trip the crew were allowed to take over the cinema for their crew-only show. We went right to the front row, which was largely vacant, and settled in. At ten to eight the ship's orchestra struck up with a medley of show numbers. They were at the back of the stage behind a curtain of fine netting which could appear to change colours or disappear according to the light controller. At precisely eight o'clock all the lights went out and the band started with a slow number.

A circle of light came on centre stage to reveal a single figure with his back to the audience, swaying slowly to the pulsating rhythm of Ravel's 'Bolero'. The solitary figure wore a black fedora hat, black jacket, trousers and carried a silver-topped black cane. The spotlight followed him as he took slow, rhythmic steps across the stage and then back again to the far side. His heavy moustache looked like a grimace. The spotlight fell to his feet and his body was lost in the blackness of the stage, as the white circle followed his feet around the rear of the stage. For a second the spotlight was cut, then reappeared in a soft pink hue. However, in that split second the figure in black, so male, so threatening, was now revealed as a woman, her long, blond hair cascading over her shoulders to the fine fabric of her diaphanous dress, which seemed to have several layers of yellow, vibrant blue, pink and red. The pace of the music had picked up almost imperceptibly, drawing the audience into each swaying movement of the dancer. The whole stage was now alive with colour, the beauty of the dancer captivating everyone in the room.

The rhythm became faster and more demanding as she removed layers of her dress, piece by piece, colour by colour, giving them to people in the audience. She dropped the vivid blue over the edge of the stage right into my lap. I was so thrilled. The remaining veils were now almost see-through and the lights softened around her until she once more held the solitary spotlight. The beautiful dancer reached to discard the last veil, but the light went out and once more we were in total blackness.

The applause was deafening. Clearly everyone in the room had been mesmerised by her performance. The spotlight came on again and there she stood in a silken black robe, her long blonde hair falling forward as she took her bows. The audience stamped their feet and clapped on. Finally, she stood erect and, to my amazement, removed her blond hair – it was a man – it was Laurie!

I couldn't believe it.

The light went out and the band started up again. After a few moments all the lights came on and someone dressed as Charlie Chaplin waddled across the stage and went into a slapstick routine. I was still stunned. The acts that followed were quite good, with lots of audience participation. Even Paddy from our cabin did a turn as a comedian, sitting on a stool telling Irish Jokes. He was funny, I was impressed. Obviously there was more to Paddy than I had imagined.

It was a good show with some excellent talent. One young winger sang a couple of songs and the audience clapped and stamped until he sang one of them again – 'Living Doll'. A few years later he became quite well known, but probably never more genuinely appreciated.

Georgina did have the final slot, but the audience had become so animated by then that not all of her words could be heard. But it was a night that everyone seemed to enjoy.

* * *

CHAPTER 21

Ceylon

At Colombo, Rachel stopped me just I was going into the mess. 'Do us a favour, Joe. Ask Toni to come with us this afternoon, but be discreet, get him on his own. He's so private, that one. Oh, and Laurie says you're both to be on the wharf by two o'clock, which means be on a tender leaving the ship by a quarter to two at the latest.'

'Okay, Rachel, but I can't answer for Toni.'

'Okay, don't worry. He'll come. So long as he thinks no one knows! We've been going out for three trips now – like an old married couple really, but he's a very private person.'

The mess was busy. All our gang were there except Reggie and Paddy. I took my lunch over and squeezed in next to Toni, but I couldn't say anything. They were arguing about which bars to go to. Chas, as usual, claimed first-hand knowledge of the carnal kind that would satisfy the most particular. Dave said, 'I know a club where the plantation owners go for fun and you won't end up with a spotty dick like you're assured of at Chas's knocking shop in Melbourne.'

Toni got up to get some coffee, so I took my mug and followed him. When we were beside the urn, I said as casually as I could, 'We're all going to Mount Lavina. Why don't you come with us, Toni?'

He closed the tap on the coffee urn and turned to face me. 'Tell me, Joe, who do you mean by "we all"?' he said, his eyes searching more for information as to just how much I was in the know.

'Oh, it's just that Laurie, Rachel, Gretchen and Gerry thought a swim might be a good idea.'

'And tell me, Joe, when did you all have this idea? Or is it something you dreamt up yourself?'

'No, no, it's just that, well, if you'd like to come, we're meeting on the wharf at two. You, me and Gerry can go ashore together and meet the others on the wharf.'

'Okay, Joe, I'll come along. The thought of one of Chas's Jack runs in this heat does nothing for me.'

Colombo Harbour was huge, with over sixty vessels moored out. Their cargo has to be transferred by lighters to the shore. In our case the cargo was passengers and they went ashore in the ship's lifeboats, six of which provided a continuous shuttle service to the wharf. In addition to the merchant ships and their cargo working, there were bum boats, of which several could be seen around most of the freighters and liners. These small vessels carried on a trade selling small items to anyone who would buy. Their offerings included silver jewellery, ivory carvings, leather wallets and crocodile skin belts. They sold diamonds, semi-precious stones and stamps. They would make you a shirt or skirt. It seemed they would supply you with anything you asked for and their persistence was amazing. If they thought there was a possible deal, be it in watches or underwear, they didn't give up. They would also function as water taxis and could cater for more exotic tastes ashore. It was amidst this cacophony of noise and acceptable discretion, as Toni later phrased it, that the six of us piled in a couple of taxis and headed out along the coast to Mt Lavinia.

I was becoming accustomed to the welcomes we received wherever we went. The concierge, resplendent in a green and gold uniform, opened the taxi doors as though we'd actually made his day the brighter. A small man in white came hurrying down the steps to greet us, his hands together as he bowed.

'Oh Mr Laurie! We are so pleased to welcome you to our establishment again.' His head went from side to side; his big brown eyes looked joyful.

'Come, come. We have your favourite drink already waiting for you!'

We were ushered through the reception area and past the dining room to the balcony bar overlooking the pool and the bay, where we could see the dhows pulled up on the beach. The Gaya Rock Hotel jutted out on the promontory, affording a spectacular view south of the bay. The shining, blue ocean came into the great curve of the bay without a wave – there was no surf at all, just the twinkling ocean arriving silently on the white, sandy beach. The palm trees reached high into the sky, their leaves shinning in the heat of the afternoon.

Laurie's double vodka and long Pimms was indeed waiting on the table, and our orders were soon delivered. I had freshly squeezed orange juice with all manner of umbrellas, cherries and lemon rings. Laurie did not approve of my drinking alcohol, except the occasional beer on board in the evening.

The man in white, who I discovered was the manager, didn't go away. In fact, on Laurie's invitation he joined us and sat down.

'Tell us, Ranji, how is the independence working out?' enquired Laurie.

'Oh, very well indeed, sir. The schools are now able to teach what we believe is good, rather than being forced to study Christianity, which, quite frankly, has a very bloody history; it is simply nor our way.'

'But you have religious friction in the north,' cut in Rachel.

'Yes, regrettably, we do. It is caused by the very vocal Islamic followers. It seems to me that wherever a religion is monotheistic, their god always has to be bigger than anyone else's.'

'Then what about your Buddha? Isn't he your God? You're no different,' insisted Rachel, warming to the subject.

Ranji laughed. 'The Buddha is not a god, nor a he. It is a natural state of awareness which we all possess to be developed. If you thought of your Christ as the good, aware side of each follower, that would be similar.'

Gretchen would not stay out of it, 'But don't you believe in many lives, and being punished now because of misdeeds in some other life?'

'I think you are referring to the teaching of karma, but the popular view of it. Simply, the law of karma is the law of cause and effect. If you don't like the ripples on the pond, stop throwing stones. The choice is yours. We really cannot blame some God, or ask him to bless the stones we throw. In Ceylon we enjoy debate on such matters. But when I was in London at the LSE, I learned that the British don't like to discuss religion, politics and sex; is that not so?'

Gretchen was fascinated with the frail-looking man who seemed so knowledgeable.

'That's right, but that's because we always take discussions personally, whereas you seem to enjoy exploring others' views.'

'Perhaps,' said Ranji. 'We should return to your original question about independence. The people are less resentful. Don't get me wrong, the British did some very good things here – our parliamentary and legal systems – but now we can govern ourselves. Did you know most people in high office here were educated in England at Oxford, Cambridge or the LSE.'

'But how will you manage in the commercial world?' asked Gretchen.

'That's no problem: we're a nation of traders – did you not see this down in the harbour?'

'Oh yes,' replied Gretchen, 'and please do not take offence. I was meaning more in the realm of international contacts. India, as your closest neighbour, must be a strong competitor.'

'Not really. You see, for a start we're still part of the Commonwealth and a member of the United Nations. We have very good contacts, and I tell you one more thing – we get to keep all the profits here in Ceylon instead of supporting a country half a world away!'

Rachel knew that Gretchen's questions were not idle, for most of her savings were invested through brokers in London, and she was always probing passengers and anyone who could help her feel out areas that might help her portfolio. Rachel wanted to develop the same skills and asked, 'Tell me Ranji, if you were investing in Ceylon, which area would you choose?'

'Well, commercially, we're expanding our tourist trade, hotels, transport, restaurants, privatised health practices and hospitals, insurance and banking. Take your pick: it's a rich and diverse country.'

And so the conversation went on for much of the afternoon. Gerry and I spent most of it in the pool whilst the others exchanged ideas, politics and aspirations. Rachel and Toni eventually slipped away.

Gerry and I were sunbathing on the loungers by the pool when he asked, 'Joe, the queens treat us so well; do you think they want our bodies? I mean, have they ever touched you?'

'No, never, and God help anyone who tried it,' I replied. 'Have you had any problems with Gretchen?'

'No, but I can't help thinking there's got to be a pay-back time, and Gretchen can be really nasty when she's upset,' said Gerry.

'The way I figure it, the queens' whole lives are on these big ships: they can lead a life they wouldn't get away with ashore, and let's face it, they're very good at their Jobs. They can't have children of their own, so some of them keep an eye out for first trippers like us, giving us time to learn the ropes. I can assure you, this is heaps better than sailing with a load of men like in my previous ship – you didn't dare turn your back on anyone.'

'So, have you ever done it with a man?' probed Gerry.

"No, not with anyone male or female,' I replied. 'Why? Have you?'

'Well, yes, sort of, in Sydney. We all went up to a dance near Chinatown and I met this girl. The following day she took me to the zoo and we did it in the woods near the wharf. Well, to be honest, I came trying to get it in, so it was really embarrassing. She wasn't impressed. I asked her if we could try later but she told me to get lost and didn't speak to me all the way back in the ferry.'

'So was that your first time?' I asked.

'Yes. Chas tried to get me off with one of his sisters in Melbourne, but I was sure I'd catch a dose, so I wouldn't go with her. I remembered the Vindi films. I don't think it's worth it.'

'Yes,' I replied. 'They were pretty awful. I must admit they stopped me trying it out.' We swam some more and, seeing Toni and Rachel return, went back over to join the others. They were discussing the merits of owning a hotel in Ceylon.

At 6pm we were called through for dinner. We sat around a large, circular table and the tastiest of dishes just keep coming. Laurie steered me through the colourful feast, avoiding those items that were over-spicy, saying, 'If you get something that's just too hot, eat some cucumber. It'll cool your mouth immediately."

It was truly wonderful. Three musicians played a sitar, tabla and a larger, upright pair of drums. With coffee they took some ganja cigarettes and let Gerry and myself have a couple of drags.

Because I didn't smoke, the first one made me cough, but by the time it came around again, I managed to get a good draw and hold it. I felt quite grown up.

A dancer came over and performed to the fast music. She weaved between the tables and was able to adopt unusual postures whilst continuing to sing – about what, I don't know; it didn't seem to matter. The evening had taken on a vibrancy that was like a magic spell, every detail perfectly clear. It seemed everyone laughed and applauded each other's wit. Toni tried to get Gretchen to do her Marlene Dietrich number, with no success. All too soon it was time to go.

'It was a terrific night, Laurie,' I said when we piled back in the cabs. 'Thank you.'

'You're very welcome, Joe. I get a kick out of seeing you enjoy yourself.'

We sped back into town, the cicadas clicking loudly all the way, and by the time we reached the wharf it was already 10.45. It was clear from the crowds of passengers and crew still waiting ashore for the ship's shuttle tenders that we were unlikely to be on board by midnight, never mind eleven, which was when crew leave finished as we were due to sail at midnight. Local traders swarmed around the waiting passengers offering them wares now at far lower prices than charged earlier in the day.

'God, this is hopeless. Come on girls, let's get a taxi,' said Laurie in frustration, and led us through to the water's edge where she financially impressed one of the local authority officials. He blew his whistle and from under the wharf appeared a water taxi. We clambered down the steps into the small launch. Others on the wharf tried to join us, but the official held them back as we sped away into the darkness. It didn't take long for others to work out the relationship between money and the official's willingness to help, and soon other taxis were loading up and leaving the wharf. Against the odds, the ship did sail on time – as always.

Sailing from Colombo harbour was very different to leaving the Australian ports. Here, we weren't alongside the wharf, so there was no fanfare or farewells, but also the tropical night was still full of activity everywhere. It made me feel we were leaving a party before the end. The strong smells of the port followed us out into the darkness until just the moon lit up our wake as we headed north-west for Aden.

* * *

CHAPTER 22

Aden / Suez / Naples

I don't know why we called at Aden; its rocky, treeless mountains contrasted with its brash shops selling cheap watches and radios. I looked up at the mountains and wondered how many British soldiers had died defending it, and why. I asked Toni, who was also looking out from the laundry deck.

'Well, Joe, it's a strategically placed harbour for the Suez Canal and the Persian Gulf, and there's a big air strip nearly, so it's an important piece of dirt.'

'It's a very ugly piece of dirt,' I replied. 'We went ashore after lunch and it was awful; no trees, no nice building, and the rancid smell was over powering.'

'Well, when your see places like this, doesn't it make you glad you don't have to live there?' Toni reflected, 'and tomorrow you've got the Red Sea and on Friday the canal. You'll know what hot is then. It's actually an interesting area – we pass, I think it's seven countries going up the Red Sea. Don't ask me to name them but you'll see some quite different cultures.'

It turned out that Toni was right. It was hot – so hot I couldn't see the other three working on the cylinder with me, the steam and the very humid air making it like working in hot clouds. Toni kept passing round the bucket of lime juice to replace the sweat that was pouring out of us. It was exhausting and Toni agreed to slow down the cylinder a bit to help us to keep going.

Halfway through the canal our convoy had to stop to allow the south-bound convoy to pass, so for about five hours we were stuck in this marine lay-by looking at a huge billboard showing a BOAC plane and a pretty hostess say, 'Get there quicker with BOAC!' – Powerful advertising that no one could miss or fail to appreciate!

'Do we get ashore in Port Said?' I asked the cloud in front of

139

me. Chas's voice replied, 'No, it's not a scheduled stop on the home run. Sometimes we do pick up a couple of passengers and of course the mail, but they come on the pilot boat. Don't worry though, you've got Naples on Monday so you can get your leg across then.'

'Is that all you ever think of Chas?' Came Pete's voice from within the cloud.

'Well, I have to go ashore for my nooky,' countered Chas.

'Just what's that supposed to mean?' came Mickey's voice, challenging.

'I was talking to Pete. No one asked you to put your oar in,' replied Chas.

'Okay, okay, break it up, you lot. It's hot and you're all a bit scratchy. Here. Get some lime into you.' The bucket came around and we filled our mugs. We drank our juice in silence and after that no one spoke for at least an hour.

* * *

Naples. At 6am the colonnades along the wharf gradually approached as the tugs nudged us gently alongside. The air was fresh, and high on a hill overlooking the city was a monastery. Naples, already bustling, seemed to bask in a grey-blue light, its pale yellow buildings crowding down to the water's edge. It was as though a drama was about to unfold any minute, Italian officials shouting at the workers, waving their arms about, and police on duty carrying revolvers.

'Don't worry, they're always like that,' said Mickey, who had joined me on the Well deck to watch us come in. 'The women are the same – it's just the way they are. Come with us at lunch time. We're eating ashore. Laurie has to do a cocktail party for the shore agents, so we're going over to a restaurant in Santa Lucia.'

'Okay, thank you. Is Gerry going?' I asked.

'Yes, of course. And don't worry about money. I'll meet you in the cabin at twelve, okay?'

I nodded gratefully, and Mickey said 'Come on, let's get down to the mess and eat. I'm starving.'

Later that morning I had to go to the cabin to get ready, and Paddy was there alone, counting an enormous pile of Italian lira, grinning from ear to ear, 'Where did you get all that from?' I asked in amazement.

He didn't reply but kept on counting the money.

The cabin door burst open and Pete and Mickey's noisy arrival came to an abrupt halt. Mouths open and eyes popping, they just stared.

'You crafty little bastard! You've been selling fags, haven't you?'

Paddy looked sheepish, but still said nothing.

'You little Irish git, you thought you'd have a piece of the action?' went on Pete.

'How much did you make, Paddy?' asked Mickey.

'A hundred and forty thousand lira, which includes my investment of about six hundred thousand lira.' Paddy started stuffing it away in his holdall again as if he thought he might lose some if he didn't stow it pronto.

Chas and Dave arrived before Paddy had got it out of sight. 'Hello, hello, what's this then? Paddy, have you been selling yourself again?' jibed Chas.

'No,' cut in Mickey, 'it seems we have a dark horse in our midst, haven't we Paddy" Come on, tell Chas how you got it.'

'Well, you all said you were going to do it,' said Paddy defiantly, 'back in Fremantle, then you all backed out, so I thought I'd better keep my mouth shut and I did it.'

'Well I never,' said Chas, pulling the top off a beer, 'apparently you turned out the smart one. I take it it's drinks all round at the Pig tonight, eh, Paddy?!'

'Oh leave him be. We can't blame him for our not doing it,' said Pete. 'Good on yer, Paddy. So tell us, how did you know who to deal with?'

'I didn't,' replied Paddy, 'but you remember you said they came on with black raincoats and empty suitcases. Well, I was just coming back from the carsie when I saw this guy in a black raincoat going along, knocking on cabin doors. I asked him what he wanted and he said he was the cigarette man, so I invited him and he offered me only a hundred thousand. I laughed and said he must think me an idiot. I think he understood and he finished up giving a hundred and forty thousand, which gives me about as much as my wages for this trip.' We all realised we'd made the same mistake. Paddy now had the respect of us all.

We took off to Santa Lucia in three black horse-drawn carriages, each horse wearing black plumes and a read flower. The L-shaped restaurant was built on a marina and designed to provide diners with a good view across to the yachts. The waiters, dressed in black and white, did not wear jackets: instead, they wore long, white aprons that came halfway up their waistcoat. They all had oily black hair and seemed to be full of their own importance. They spoke only Italian, and that very quickly, so we all had Bolognaise and Chianti. This was my first time ashore with the lads since Sydney. I noticed the difference. Whereas Laurie was fluent in Italian, French and German, and we wouldn't have felt so much like second class citizens. But for all that, we enjoyed the food and the violinist who went from table to table playing 'Take me Back to Sorrento'. I couldn't look up and had no money to give him. Paddy did the honours, and in fact paid for the whole meal, which further impressed everyone. Opposite the restaurant was parked a beautiful speedboat with highly polished mahogany decking and chrome fittings. I wondered if it belonged to the big house with the word Eldorado on it, and thought of some ice cream in England called Eldorado.

'Hey Chas, do you think that's the home of the Eldorado ice cream man?'

'I don't know Joe, but ice cream is an Italian invention isn't it, so it may be.'

We walked back to the ship, looking at the shops and cars. Young boys stopped us to ask if we wanted their sister. Their sister asked if we wanted her brother. The brother asked 'You wanna my mother?' It appeared everyone had to turn a sov.

* * *

142

CHAPTER 23

The Channels

We sailed at five o'clock and Reggie and Dave were on the well deck with me, watching us slide away from the wharf.

'Your missus will be getting excited for your home coming, won't she Reggie?' asked Dave. 'She'll have to kick out the lodger for a couple of weeks!'

'I don't suppose you've ever met any decent folk,' smiled Reggie. 'Not everyone is leaping about from bed to bed you know.'

'Hey, hey, hey – don't be so serious. I was only kidding,' said Dave, mimicking someone suffering many blows. 'You see those cranes?' he went on, a quick change of subject being the best defence. 'Well, this morning when they were unloading the disembarking passengers' luggage onto some baggage trolleys with high wire sides. Well, occasionally a group of cases went in-between and down to a lower level, like some passengers were not going to get their luggage – it was going to be spirited away.'

'You know what that was, don't you?' said Reggie. 'Like, did you see the men in the black raincoats?'

'Well yes. There was one always around, but I thought he was security,' answered Dave, not willing to admit that a Geordie might know something a Cockney didn't about the way the world works; his curiosity blatantly showing, nevertheless.

'They're the Mafia, the guys who buy up all the cigarettes they can – that's how they get them ashore. They're Paddy's mates.'

'I don't think Paddy would like to hear you call the Mafia his mates,' I chipped in.

'Well that's the bloody reality of it. Who does he think he's dealing with?' Reggie asked, not waiting for an answer. 'Cigarettes aren't the only thing they buy, you know. They buy booze, passports, drugs and anything they can flog. Paddy reckoned they offered him ten quid for his passport!'

'He didn't sell it, did he?' I asked.

'No, you must be kidding. That Paddy is no bloody fool,' said Dave, begrudgingly.

The tugs let us go, and our ship's horn blasted three times to bid farewell to the cranes and yellow buildings as we slowly gathered speed and headed south-west for the straits of Gibraltar and England. The Mediterranean was like yellow silk in the evening light. We went below and joining the others at the cinema for Jack Hawkins in 'The Cruel Sea'.

* * *

I was very excited as we passed the Ushant light and entered the England Channel. It was dark, and as yet I could not make out any lights to port, but tomorrow we would be in Tilbury and home.

I couldn't help thinking back to when I sailed down the Channel, and all that had happened since. It seemed a lifetime ago but in fact it was only eight months; tomorrow would be the first of April 1954, and in just over four weeks I would be sixteen. I had absolutely no idea of where I was headed from here.

The cold wind soon put a stop to my looking for the lights of England and I went below to the Pig. It was packed and obviously I wasn't the only one with the Channels. The atmosphere was buoyant with the crown and anchor board was making heaps. I found Chas and watched him make exactly ten shillings then stop. 'Toni would be proud of you,' I observed.

I went to the cabin to pack my things and realised that was only a five minute job. I had inherited some nice shirts and Gretchen had given me a blue shirt she'd enthusiastically bought whilst half cut in 'Frisco' and regretted when sober. I thought it was just smashing, and would wear it to go home tomorrow. Laurie had taken up the trousers a little and it fitted well. Even though I hadn't received a wage, the kindness of the guys in the cabin and Laurie, Gretchen and Rachel meant I had been better looked after than at any previous time and had some great gear. I was so excited. 'I doubt I can sleep,' I said to Gerry when he came into the cabin.

'Well, most of them won't sleep; they'll be drinking all night, so you might not get much sleep anyway.'

Just then Laurie came in. 'Now then, you two, come up to our cabin at eleven o'clock and have a drinky-poos with us. Just for half an hour, then get your heads down. You've got a big day tomorrow. I don't want you getting into any of those all night piss-ups – is that clear?'

'Yes Laurie,' we replied in unison.

'I mean it!'

'Yes Laurie,' we said again, smiling. She left.

'What are we going to do until then?' Gerry asked.

'Well there's always the mess. Let's go and see what we can scrounge.'

We finished up with a plate of sausage and mashed potatoes, some beetroot and a big wedge of cake each, which we devoured as we discussed with full mouths what we were going to do first when we got home. We washed down the food with a pint of tea each then, with blankets around our shoulders, we went through to the laundry deck aft to look for lights in the Channel. We stayed for over an hour, but apart from passing ships we saw nothing.

Promptly at 11pm we knocked on Laurie's door. Rachel opened it wearing a full-length floral dress. She looked like she was off to a picnic. She urged us in quickly, as though she didn't want the neighbours to see.

'Laurie's not down yet, but take a seat. She won't be long.'

Rachel poured us rum and Coke without asking and heaped in lots of ice. 'Are you excited about getting in tomorrow?' she asked.

'You bet,' said Gerry. 'My girl friend will be waiting for me.'

'And what about you, Joe? Do you have a girl friend waiting?'

'No, but my mum will be pleased to see me – I hope!' I said, not sure what sort of reception I might get. I rather suspected I was in for a telling off, at least.

The cabin door opened and Laurie came in, shutting the door, shedding her stiff white jacket and pouring a large gin seemingly all

145

in one move.

'Now, you two, has Rachel been looking after you?'

'Yes thanks,' answered Gerry. Laurie looked at me.

'Yes, yes of course, Laurie. Rum and Coke as we came through the door!'

'Good,' said Laurie, satisfied. 'Now, we've bought you each a little prezzie,' Reaching under her pillow, she withdrew two small parcels wrapped in shiny red paper.

'Can we open them now?' I asked.

'Yes, of course,' said Rachel, caught up in the excitement.

We both ripped off the coloured paper on our presents to reveal watches! Gerry's was all gold and very flash; mine was chrome with a black leather strap, which I thought much smarter. I didn't know what to say. I just kept looking at it.

Gerry soon recovered. 'Where did you buy this?'

'In Aden. We thought you'd like it,' said Rachel.

'It's terrific,' said Gerry seriously. 'Hey thanks, you guys.'

'And what about you, O silent one?' said Laurie.

'Did you buy this in Aden as well?'

'No,' replied Laurie. 'If you must know, a punter bought it out of the ship's shop and gave it to me as a present. I've got too many watches and I thought you'd like it. It's a Girard Pirregaux. It's okay. Do you like it?'

'Like it? It's really smashing. I don't know what to say. Thank you. You're very kind. You've done so much for me since I joined in Sydney. I can't, I mean I don't know, I've never – thanks, Laurie.'

Laurie stood up and collected the discarded wrapping paper. 'Here. Let me refresh your drinks.'

I think she was pleased in her own way; she seemed a little embarrassed.

I put on my new watch and Gerry put on his. The conversation was a little difficult.

'Well, now. Are you two coming back next trip?' asked Laurie.

Gerry said 'Yes'. I said I didn't know. I'd love to, but I wasn't sure of my mum's reaction and how the Child Welfare would view my jumping ship.

'Well, you take of yourself, Joe. You're a good lad with some good qualities; don't let people put you down.' We had hugs all round and return to our cabin quite squizzy. They had been a bit heavy-handed with the drinks. However, that proved a blessing: we both slept through till almost dawn, despite some raucous partying in nearby cabins.

At 6am I was awake and, grabbing my trousers and T-shirt, was up on the well deck in a flash to see us coming in. We were already alongside, gangways down and officials milling around.

The vista of port buildings was drab and grey in the cold morning half-light, but still magical for all that, and I couldn't wait to get ashore. Tilbury would not be considered scenically appealing, but England it still was, and for all the beauties of other countries, one's own country, no matter how drab, can seem wonderful. However, it was freezing. Our T-shirts gave no protection against the cold dawn, so we couldn't survive topside: we would have to take it in small doses.

We ducked down below and along to the mess for some good hot tea.

The laundry was closed. Apparently all the linen went ashore under contract, so we were free to go after we'd scrubbed out the laundry and when we cleared our papers. Since I wasn't having to queue for pay, that should be easy. Other crew members had to sign off articles and collect wages.

After breakfast we turned to and scrubbed out the laundry in record time, finishing by 9.20. When I returned to the cabin there was a note for me to report to the bridge – presumably to collect my shilling of wages!

The bridge was deserted except for two customs men and the Mate poring over some manifests.

'Where's the captain?' I enquired.

'Try his cabin.' the Mate said brusquely. I went to his cabin and knocked softly.

'Yes, come,' the voice answered from inside. I opened the door and gingerly poked my head in.

'Oh, you're Lawson, aren't you?'

'Yes, sir.'

'Well, now. Have you enjoyed the trip?' the captain asked.

'Yes, sir.'

'And you're glad to be home, no doubt,'

'Yes, sir.'

'The chief has given you a good report, said you worked well. I just wanted to tell you that if you want to return next trip, we'd be pleased to have you. If you want to do that, ring Leadenhall Street by next Wednesday. However, before then, because you're still under sixteen, you come under the jurisdiction of the Children's Welfare and they'll want to see you in your home town. Nottingham isn't it?'

'Yes, sir.'

'Well, here's your book. You've got a VNC in it, which is a shame, but not the end of the world. Here's a railway warrant from Tilbury to Nottingham, and here is one pound to go in your pocket.'

'Thank you, sir.'

'Right. Off you go, and good luck. Remember you must report to Child Welfare straight away.'

'Yes, sir. Thank you sir.' I was down the stairs to the cabin in double-quick time. There was no one there. I wondered if they were queuing for their pay or had gone. There was nothing else to do. Oh well, here we go, on the road again; and gripping my carrier bag firmly, I went ashore for the last time.

On the station, though it was packed and the train full, I saw no one I recognised. I changed at St Pancras for the Nottingham train and still saw no familiar faces. I sat quietly, looking at people's back gardens as they dashed past my window. They looked monotonous and ordinary – yes, I could do with some ordinary. This was it.

I thought of the others, all going their different ways, and felt the acute finality of the parting: no long goodbyes, no 'let's write', just another ending without words, without remorse, another horizon to go to, and a sort of mutually agreed severing of a relationship. I felt hollow. Yet it was no good wasting time on such thoughts – on to the next horizon.

We finally arrived at Nottingham station, and the ordinariness of life in the midlands returned in full force. I soon found a bus and drank in the familiar smells and passing streets. Everything was so black: soot covered all the buildings. Eventually we came into our road and I jumped off the bus, ran all the way to the house where my mother lived, pushed open the gate and went through to knock on the back door.

She finally answered. On seeing me, she stood there speechless. I was shocked – how small she had become, and so much older looking.

'Well, are you going to stand there all day?' she asked when she found voice.

She was sober, I was relieved and happy. I climbed the three steps and went in.

'You've grown – let's look at you. Where did you get that suit? It's dreadful! The Children's Welfare wants to see you. Tomorrow will do. I'll ring and tell them you've arrived. Why didn't you write? I've been worried! It's not easy, you know.'

'No, mum.'

Later I went out to see if I could find Barrie or Peter, or any of my other playmates. No: it seemed they were all busy living their lives. Except Barrie, the only one I could find, said, 'Hello, when did you get back? How long are you home for?' This, I was to learn, was usually the absolute limit of people's interest in where I'd been or what I'd been up to.

The following morning I presented myself to the Welfare Committee at ten sharp, my mum making sure I went – and that I was dressed in what she felt was proper clothes.

Three people made up the committee: two ladies and a man who was all tweeds and leather patches. They asked a lot of questions about why I had jumped ship, and I seemed to be answering for hours. Actually, they weren't bad; it was just that mum was sitting in also, and I wasn't sure how much she should hear. It reached a sort of crescendo when they asked, as with one voice, 'Tell me, Joe. Are you still a virgin? In every sense of the word. I am sure you know what we mean.'

'Yes of course. And yes, I'm still a virgin.' They all sighed with relief – as though their pension had just been confirmed.

'Joe, did you have any special friends on board?'

'My heroes were the bosun and the mate; they were terrific. As for special friends, yes, but when you leave the ship, they've gone.'

Anyway, they sat back together and said I was not going to be permitted to return to sea. They had a position for me in ' private service' which, they felt, would keep me away from undesirable influences – which just goes to show how much they knew!

-          *The End*   -

Footnote: Joe went back to sea a number of years later and served on a number of famous liners.

# # #

Glossary

Adrift – late for duties

Aft – going from bow to stern

Bevvies – drinks

Blues – navy blue uniform of the northern climes

Book – Seaman's passport and records

Boxed off – cleaned away

BR – bedroom steward

Bulkhead – ship walls

Cabin – Cabin boy

Carsie – toilet

Channels – the excitement of approaching home waters

Crown and Anchor – a simplified version of roulette

DBS – Distressed British Seamen

Deckhead – ceiling

Dhobiing – washing clothes

Donkey greaser – greases and oils the engine constantly – usually blacks

Dummy – sideboard

Fast on – asleep

Fiddles – table edging, raised to prevent crockery going adrift

Flying Angel – Mission to Seamen (club)

Galley – galley (kitchen) boy

Guns – gonorrhoea

Hard tack – uncooked food

Mate – first officer

Perks breakfast – free meals for shore side officials

Portside – left side facing forward

Samuel Everite – watch

Sarnies – sandwiches

Second – second steward

Scuttlebutt – shipboard gossip

Starboard – right side of the ship facing forward

Strapping up – clearing away

Sub – an advance on your wage account onboard

Tabnabs – small biscuits/cakes

The Pig – crew bar

Turn to – report for work

U Gang – general duties squad

VNC – voyage not completed

Vindi – the training ship Vindicatrix

Winger – table steward

* * *

Discover other titles by Warren Karno at
www.amazon.com

The Grapple and The Guinea Pig (e-book)
Double Take (e-book)
Dangerous Friends (e-book and paperback)

* * *

About the Author

Warren Karno, spent many years at sea before becoming an hotelier, and involved in the Banking/Investment industry. Now retired, he spends his time working with charities; travelling and pursuing his passion for writing and oil painting.

* * *

Connect with Me Online

www.warrenkarno.com or portfolio.press@xtra.co.nz

* * *

11291554R00086

Printed in Great Britain
by Amazon.co.uk, Ltd.,
Marston Gate.